YOUR MARRIAGE

John F. DeYonker, D.O.

Thomas E. Tobin, C.SS.R.

LIGUORI
PUBLICATIONS

One Liguori Drive
Liguori, Missouri 63057
(314) 464-2500

TO THE
MEMORY OF

Dr. Francis DeYonker
and
Father Thomas E. Tobin
dedicated
marriage counselors

Imprimi Potest:
Edmund T. Langton, C.SS.R.
Provincial, St. Louis Province
Redemptorist Fathers

Imprimatur:
+ George J. Gottwald
Vicar General, Archdiocese of St. Louis

Revised Edition 1979
Library of Congress Catalog Card Number: 68-57211
ISBN 0-89243-059-1
Printed in U.S.A.

table of contents

preface

It is truly important to know that our whole society is dependent upon the stability and the strength of our family system. It is undoubtedly too much to say that we have a sick society because there are certainly definite areas of strength and well-being at all levels. However, there are many unhealthy areas and family life is one of them.

Much more could be done to eliminate unhappy marriages prior to the marriage date itself. There is a developing interest in family life education for high school and elementary schools. There is a tremendous drive to get whatever is meant by sex education into our school systems. Outside of the Church, which provides premarriage courses or Pre-Cana Conferences or some kind of preparation, society generally is spending more money to prepare youngsters to drive automobiles than to prepare for marriage. For this reason, we believe that any amount of energy expended on premarriage instructions is going to be worthwhile and if these energies are brought together from interprofessional points of view, involving the physical, psychological, social, and spiritual relationship, perhaps a good number of people can be helped to avoid many of the possible pitfalls. Furthermore, much more can be done to promote a relationship that is like the relationship between Christ and the Church and one, therefore, that will bring couples the happiness they so ardently expect.

Many marriages begin to fail "right from the start." When interviewing people who are contemplating separation or divorce or who are seeking marital counseling, they indicate their problems started right from the beginning or the very early part of marriage.

There are many reasons for this kind of a disintegrating process in the relationship which should be growing. Some of these reasons are: lack of maturity on the part of one or both parties; lack of a basic love relationship; ignorance of how to adjust to marriage and to one another; perhaps too strong a relationship with a father or mother which now cannot be cut off, or perhaps the parents will not cut the strings allowing their children freedom and independence to develop a mature life; or other reasons which, if present and are not handled correctly, will result in unhappiness even if the marriage endures.

This book is meant for those preparing for marriage — to help them to understand some of the problems that may arise and how to cope with them; and for those already married — to help them to solve problems that may exist in their present marriage. Another important reason to justify this book, because we believe it aims directly at the bond of relationship between a man and a woman, is to make the expectations of two people more practical and possible of attainment. Also, it attempts to lessen the gap between the theology of the Church on marriage and the present reality of marriage.

St. Paul's beautiful passage in his Letter to the Ephesians where he compares the relationship between husband and wife to the relationship between Christ and the Church must be considered in its entire context — especially in today's world. Our culture looks on marriage as a partnership where dialogue, equal dignity, shared ideals, and common search for what is true, good, and helpful are important factors in married life. St. Paul says, "Be subject to one another out of reverence for Christ" (Eph 5:21).

There ought to be a very serious attempt to try to make people understand what is meant when they hear the words that no greater happiness can be found in this vale of tears than that which is promised to the newly married. This kind of happiness will result only when there is a basic selfless love for one another, and when this love is based on a mutual love of God, and his love in turn is used to love one another, so that two people love one another in Christ and Christ in one another. Together in Christ they go to the Father and his love comes back to them in ever-increasing amounts. However, this is not an automatic process. This does not happen simply because two people have married before a priest and two witnesses with a Mass and a social celebration. This does not happen unless two people, emotionally healthy, strive to promote a degree of friendship and a love of friendship in which they can truly exemplify, to some degree, that kind of relationship which must exist between Christ and his Church. Without this relationship, it appears as a sort of mockery to call such an empty union a valid Christian marriage.

It is our hope that those who make use of this book will profit from the suggestions offered here and will try to make certain that many of the obstacles that might have been present can be eliminated by their own thoughtfulness and concern for them. On the other hand, they will put into practice in a loving concern for one another, positive factors which are often omitted.

We in family life work and marriage counseling are most grateful to the late Dr. John DeYonker who supplied the original draft of this book, and to the Rev. Thomas E. Tobin, who added much from his own knowledge and experience, and put it in its present form.

Very Rev. Msgr. Clifford P. Sawher
Director of Family Life Bureau
Archdiocese of Detroit

NOTICE TO READERS

Throughout this book, pronouns that refer to masculine or feminine (for example, ''he'' or ''she,'' ''his'' or ''her'') are often interchangeable unless, of course, they refer to an obviously male or female characteristic.

introduction

Congratulations to you on your approaching marriage! It is the most important step that you will take in your life. This book presents tips and pointers from the experience of a psychiatrist and a priest counselor. It is not a theoretical book but a practical guide to help you realize the full potential for happiness that can be found in marriage.

Important

Your marriage is so important because so much depends on it. Happy family life is the backbone of healthy neighborhood, government, and Church life. As the family is, so are all other communities.

Your own happiness is closely connected with what you give and find in marriage. The Church promises that you will have "the greatest measure of earthly happiness that may be allotted to man in this vale of tears." But this promise is realized only "if true love and the unselfish spirit of perfect sacrifice guide your every action." You must enter marriage not so much to receive as to give. True love makes you want to bring happiness to your partner in marriage. If you think primarily of yourself, "What can I get from marriage?" you will get only yourself and will be miserable because no one finds happiness in selfishly thinking and doing only for himself. Happiness is not directly sought and attained. It is a by-product of duty and love. When you try to make the other happy you suddenly realize that you are happy yourself. Christ taught this lesson long ago: "He that shall lose his life shall find it" (Mt 10:39).

On your wedding day you will make a lifelong commitment. An instruction on marriage, still pertinent today, says, "This union then is most serious because it will bind you together for life in a relationship so close and so intimate that it will profoundly influence your whole future. That future, with its hopes and disappointments, its successes and failures, its pleasures and its pains, its joys and its sorrows, is hidden from your eyes. You know that these elements are mingled in every life and so are to be expected in your own. . . . You take each other for better or for worse, for richer or for poorer, in sickness and in health, until death.''

Love intensifies joys and lessens sorrows. Loneliness is the great anguish of man and you are not alone in marriage. You cannot be unhappy in the midst of those who love and care for you. In the security of love you can grow as a person. A home can be made into a Church in miniature in which there is human and divine love and joy. Happily married people easily understand the words of Edgar Guest: ''It takes a heap of living to make a house a home.''

Unhappy Marriages

There is no need to emphasize the fact that many people are unhappily married. Many of these marriages are broken in the divorce court; many others stay together ''for the sake of the children.'' In our counseling experience it always bothers us to meet so many men and women who have not found true happiness and contentment in their marriages. They limp through life when there is no real necessity for doing so. Bickering and nagging, coldness and indifference, a turning away to other persons or other interests, a desire to hurt rather than help — all these evils and more are found in unhappy marriages.

Children

Your children will need well-adjusted and happy parents so that they can develop into mature and self-reliant men and women. Parents who love each other and their children freely give themselves to the children. Children feel they are loved and protected by many proofs of love which range from affection to provision for all their needs. Children in unhappy marriages sense and feel the unhappiness. Their parents are so absorbed in their own problems that they are not able to care for the children. So often children carry scars from their childhood into their own marriages. These scars can be overcome by understanding and effort but they are real scars which should not be there.

Eternity

The importance of your marriage goes beyond time into eternity. Marriage is not only a school of human but also divine love. By prayer, good example, and mutual encouragement, and above all in the atmosphere of love, you will learn to love God more and serve him better. In the sacrament of Matrimony Christ also pledges you his all-powerful assistance to overcome difficulties and to grow in love for each other and for him. When love reigns in a home it is much easier to find God.

To Know and Love

The purpose of this book is to help you to know and love yourself and each other, as well as to explain the privileges and responsibilities of marriage. As intelligent persons you must know before you act; you must not jump blindly into the darkness. To love wisely depends on knowledge.

You must first of all know yourself. You are a unique human person who differs from all others. You have your own personal strengths to be developed and weaknesses to be controlled. Do not try to duck problems; face and solve them. Get professional help if necessary. Do not try to bury any living problem. Only dead problems can be safely buried. Live problems do not remain buried but disturb in many open and hidden ways.

You must also know your future partner. Do not see him/her through a romantic haze that clouds your vision. There is a tendency to see only what you want to see. Sometimes this is done unconsciously so that you are not aware that you are refusing to take an honest look at the other. Don't take things for granted; talk about everything before your marriage. The best way to know is by talking, freely and openly, on anything and everything that could have even the smallest bearing on your future life together.

There is much to be learned about marriage before you enter it. There are many responsibilities that must be known and realized before you are able to make the decision whether you are mature enough to marry. It is good to know the many positive ways in which you can make your marriage better, as well as the possible pitfalls that can harm your marriage.

To Love

Since marriage is a "community of love" you must understand the nature of love and the signs of true love. First of all, you must love yourself. If you do not love yourself you are not capable of loving anyone else. Remember that you "must love your neighbor as yourself." Only when you see yourself as a real person worthy of being loved can you offer yourself to your partner in love. You would never believe him when he told you that he loved you because you could never see anything lovable in yourself. When you love yourself you can see your partner as lovable and really love him. Love has to be a person-to-person response to each other. To love yourself also means to forgive yourself for any mistakes or sins. Human persons are not perfect and do fall. The good God understands human weakness and does forgive and forget. Follow his example.

True love is neither mere physical attraction nor romantic feelings but a reasonable gift of yourself to one who will make a good marriage partner. Love is reasonable, not blind. Blind eyes can be jolted open by the realities of marriage responsibilities and the inability of one or the other to accept and fulfill these responsibilities. Make sure your future partner loves you and is capable not only of lofty promises but also fulfillment. Some people are high on promises and short on action.

The purpose of these pages is to help you know and love each other and to understand the obligations of marriage so that you will have a very happy marriage. Prepare, prepare, know what you are doing and do not jump into marriage but walk slowly and carefully.

Perhaps the newly married or those not so newly married might find in these pages a fresh insight or a needed reminder of a forgotten truth to help make their marriage even better.

PART 1
MARRIAGE

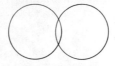

vocation
purposes
sacrament

chapter 1
vocation

You are about to make a choice that will change your whole way of life. You will no longer be a single man or woman but a married man or woman; you will leave your parents' home and begin your own home with each other. There will be new obligations, new privileges that will profoundly affect your lives.

Marriage is a true vocation, a stable and permanent way of life with its basic structure determined by God who instituted marriage. Vocation comes from the Latin word which means "calling." It is used to designate a basic way of life such as the priestly or married state.

Love God

A good way to understand your vocation of marriage is to place it in the framework of your primary vocation to love God. This is the call which God repeats many times in the Bible and in the hearts of individuals. "You shall love the Lord, your God, with your whole heart, your whole soul and your whole mind. This is the greatest and the first commandment" (Mt 22:37-38).

God calls you to love him by the important facts of your creation and redemption.

Out of love God created you as the special person you are. True love always desires to give, to share. Before time began the Father, Son, and Holy Spirit determined to share their life and love with you. As God tells us in the Old Testament: "With an everlasting love have I loved you" (Jer 31:3). It is very important to realize that God loves you as a distinct individual. You are a particular aspect of God's perfection shared by no other person. You have something that you alone can give to God, the gift of yourself. The words of St. Augustine are still so true: "You have made us for yourself, O Lord, and restless is our heart until it rests in you."

The second reason why you are called to love God is because Christ redeemed you. "For God so loved the world that he gave his only-begotten Son that those who believe in him may have life everlasting" (Jn 3:16). With Christ you died to sin and rose to a new life. You are made one with Christ in his Mystical Body and can rightfully with Christ call upon God as your Father.

The Married Vocation

Your vocation in life is marriage. You are called to love God through the love that you have for each other and for your future children. This means that you do not go to God alone but together. Your human love for each other comes from God and leads to him. One of the great Catholics of the nineteenth century was Frederick Ozanam, the founder of the St. Vincent de Paul Society. This prayer was frequently on his lips: "God grant that my wife may be better and holier through me and I better and holier through her."

Marriage is a call to share in God's creative love. True love always wishes to share and give. God shared his perfections with you by creating you. Men and women share in God's creative power by becoming fathers and mothers. Marriage is a trinity of the husband, wife, and God. All three cooperate in the conception of a child. The father and mother give part of themselves, the seed and the egg, and God infuses an immortal soul. It is well to know that the souls do not exist before the body in the sense that the souls are already created and waiting for bodies. A soul is created only when a man and woman prepare the body for its reception.

Is Marriage My Vocation?

Perhaps, you may be wondering if marriage is really your vocation or if you really love your partner. You may be asking yourself this question: "How can I know?" This is a very good question which should be asked and answered before marriage. God will not send a special message to assure you one way or the other, but he will help you find the right answer.

There really are two questions to be answered: Is marriage your vocation? Is marriage to this person your vocation?

Is marriage your vocation? This depends on whether you are capable of fulfilling your role in marriage as husband and father, or wife and mother, and also have the desire to marry. A person might want marriage but be incapable of carrying out the duties of marriage, or might be capable of being a good marriage partner but have no desire to marry. In either case marriage would be disastrous. A man or woman who is mature, unselfish, and able to get along with others has the basic qualities needed for marriage. The desire to marry must be an intelligent and wholehearted response to the values seen in marriage.

With This Person?

Hopefully you have dated more than one person so that you have an idea of the kind of partner you want and need. Also, dating several people should have helped you grow as a person and in your ability to relate well with the opposite sex.

Then your choice settled on one. Perhaps, you were first attracted by the external appearance, which led you to desire to know the person better. As you dated you began to like and then love each other. To like means to find good qualities which you value in the other. A husband and wife must have many qualities in common so that they can fit together as a team. If they share the same faults there can be real trouble; if they share the same good qualities there will be much happiness. Two aggressive persons will fight and hurt each other; an aggressive partner may drive a shy person more and more into his shell; two loving and self-giving persons will bring much joy and success to their marriage.

This liking turned into love when you not only wanted

to receive from the other but also to give yourself to him or her. You wanted to be with each other. You thought about each other when absent, planned little surprises, desired to share your joys and sorrows with each other. You were thrilled at the thought of having children together. You wanted to be seen with each other; you looked forward without fear of boredom to many happy years together.

This person was your choice and you were certain of it. You are then ready to give yourself to each other and say, "I love you." "I love you alone." "I will love you forever." "My vocation is to love you."

chapter 2

purposes

On the eve of your marriage it is important to ask yourself why you are getting married. A serious step in life demands serious reasons. It is not good to take the reasons for granted. Bring them to the surface of your mind and take a long and hard look at them. Make sure you are doing the right thing for the right reasons.

The first answer probably will be: "I love him," "I love her." This surely is the best of answers if you understand what true love is. But blind infatuation and unreal romance can masquerade as true love and proclaim: "Love conquers all." Unfortunately it does not.

Sometimes a person marries just to get away from home. Or perhaps many classmates are already married with their families started and one gets a bit anxious. It might be that a romance has been broken and the person wants to marry on the rebound. Sometimes the desire for physical sex could be so overpowering that a couple figures that they had better marry soon. Again a person might be tempted to marry even without love of the other, but just for financial security. Another person might just be tired of being asked: "When are you going to get married?'' or feel strange as the only single person in the midst of married friends. These are only some of the wrong reasons that lead persons to marry.

God's Purposes

At the beginning of this book it is well to examine the purposes God had in mind when he instituted marriage. These can be learned from the Bible and the official documents of the Church.

Two reasons for marriage are children and companionship. God implanted the instinct for sex and the desire for marriage in man and woman so that children would be born and raised as his children. Companionship (or the need and desire for companionship) leads to the conception and care of children.

The Bible

The first two chapters of Genesis clearly explain God's intentions in instituting marriage.

"God created man in his image. In the image of God he created him. Male and female he created them. Then God blessed them and said to them, be fruitful and multiply; fill the earth and subdue it'' (Gn 2:27-28). God made man and woman so that in their love they might unite and fill the earth. Eve understood this plan of God when she said: "I have given birth to a manchild with the help of the Lord'' (Gn 4:1).

The personal aspect of companionship is evident in this oft-quoted passage: "It is not good that man be alone; I will make him a helper like unto himself — for this reason a man shall leave his father and mother and cling to his wife and the two shall become one flesh.'' (Gn 2:18-24).

The Purposes

For many centuries Catholic theology distinguished between the primary and secondary ends of marriage. The primary was the procreation and education of children. Parenthood in the full sense of the conception and care of children was the first end of marriage. The

secondary ends were mutual aid, a relief of sexual desire, and the fostering of mutual love. These secondary ends were held as subordinate or of secondary importance in relation to the primary ends.

Vatican II

In recent years many theologians have emphasized the personal love aspect of marriage. They have not denied the procreative purpose but have maintained that the importance of personal love has been cast into the shadows by the overemphasis of the social or procreative purpose. They feel that in these days of personalism when people are very conscious of their own value as distinct individuals and not just faceless numbers lost in a crowd that the personal or love values should be stressed.

It is interesting that Vatican II made a deliberate effort to avoid using the words primary and secondary. The document clearly recognized the two basic purposes of marriage, but usually joined them together.

"For God himself is the author of Matrimony, endowed as it is with various benefits and purposes. All of these have a very decisive bearing on the continuation of the human race, on the personal development and eternal destiny of the individual members of a family, and on the dignity, stability, peace, and prosperity of the family itself and of human society as a whole. By their very nature, the institution of Matrimony itself and conjugal love are ordained for the procreation and education of children, and find in them their ultimate crown" *(Church in the Modern World,* n. 48).

Pius XI

This teaching of the personal goals and values of marriage was foreshadowed by a well-known passage in an encyclical by Pope Pius XI. "This mutual interior formation of the partners, this earnest desire of perfecting one another, can be said in a certain very true sense, as the Roman Catechism teaches, to be the primary cause and reason of marriage — if only marriage is taken not strictly as an institution for the proper procreation and rearing of children, but in a broader sense as a sharing, a community, a union of their whole life'' *(Chaste Wedlock,* n. 24).

Think about your reasons for marriage; talk them over with each other. Ask God to enlighten your mind to know the real reasons and to strengthen your will to make the proper decision.

chapter 3
sacrament

Christ visited and sanctified the marriage of the young couple at Cana. He will come to your wedding in the sacrament of Matrimony. Just as the young couple needed faith to see Christ in his bodily presence, so you will need faith to see Christ in his sacramental presence. But he will be truly present at your wedding.

A Sacrament

During his lifetime men and women came into contact with Christ in the flesh. Now people come into contact with the risen and glorified Christ through various signs that represent him. We cannot see Christ, but we can see the Church which is a sign or sacrament of Christ. We do not hear Christ's words in our ears nor see his hand raised in forgiveness, but he comes into our lives through the sacraments. Our faith teaches us that Christ is present under the appearance of bread and wine, that it is really his hand raised in absolution over our sins. Thus a sacrament is a visible sign instituted by Christ to give invisible grace. In the sacraments we encounter Christ.

Sacrament of Matrimony

Every marriage of Christians is a sacrament, a sign of

human and divine love. When you stand at the altar and speak your marriage vows you not only show your human love but also give divine love to each other. You are the ministers, the ones who actually give the sacrament of Matrimony. In the other sacraments, with the exception of emergency Baptism, a priest or a bishop confers the sacrament. But in marriage the man and woman give the sacrament; the priest, best man, and bridesmaid are the official witnesses of the sacred ceremony you perform. You will bring Christ closer to your partner by giving the sacrament of Matrimony.

The words you will speak are the signs of your love and gift of yourself to the other. This love which unites you together is also a sign or image of the love which unites Christ and his Church.

Sacramental Grace

In marriage you are united to Christ in a special way as Christian husband and wife. In other words the sacrament of Matrimony brings sanctifying grace as well as special matrimonial graces. Grace is a gift of God. Sanctifying grace is the gift by which God adopts you as a child and gives you a share in his divine life. It makes you a brother or sister of Christ.

The special matrimonial graces are gifts that unite you to each other and to Christ as Christian husband and wife and bestow the right to all the actual graces needed to live as a Christian husband and wife.

Matrimonial graces help to overcome the selfishness that is so much a part of fallen human nature. Selfishness puts you first and makes you regard the other merely as a thing to be used, not as a person with his or her own dignity and value. Original sin turned us away from God and others and inward on ourselves. Since marriage means that two people are to become one it is necessary that selfishness be controlled and that the married person be directed to the other.

One of the effects of original sin was that the order between the various elements of the human person was disturbed. Thus the human will lost its complete control over the sexual instinct. In fallen man the sexual instinct can seek sex as an "it," only as a pleasure to be selfishly enjoyed either with one's partner or with someone else. Matrimonial grace helps to direct the sexual instinct away from others and toward each other. It also makes the sexual instinct the expression of true human love.

Elevates Love

The sacramental grace of marriage also elevates the human love of the husband and wife for each other and their children. Christ called love of neighbor "my commandment." In Christian marriage the husband and wife love each other not only with a human but also a Christian love. In a very special sense the partner is the neighbor! It is difficult to fully understand all the mystery contained in the sacrament of Matrimony. But you are united to each other not only as husband and wife. Thus marriage is not two but three persons, a trinity of lovers, the husband and wife and Christ who is the most loving and powerful member of the trinity.

Right to Help

The sacramental grace of Matrimony brings with it special sacramental grace to help assist you in living your married life. In a practical way this means that you have a right to the actual graces of God needed to be a good husband or wife, father or mother. It is important to realize that actual grace only aids you to act as a Christian husband, wife, father, or mother. It is not something magical which does everything for you. It helps you to help yourself. When Christ met you in the sacrament of Matrimony he promised to give you all the assistance that you would need. In a practical way this assistance is light for the mind and courage for the will.

Light for the Mind

This divine light will brighten many areas of your life. It may be the problem of choosing the right job which is so important for the financial needs of the family as well as the long-term personal satisfaction of the husband. Or light may be needed to decide whether a certain house is in the right location and within the proper price range. At times a certain tension or misunderstanding may come into your life — perhaps a tension which you are not able to handle. You may not know how to talk to a certain child, you may have a sick baby and not be able to contact a doctor, you may not know what is wrong and what should be done. In all these matters God expects you to use your own mind, but perhaps when you are befuddled and confused suddenly a ray of light may come. You don't quite know why it is there but you know that it is there. It is the special effect of the sacrament of Matrimony.

Courage for the Will

Light for the mind is necessary but even more so is courage for the will. Knowledge of itself does not necessarily lead to action. The difficulty so often is not in the field of knowledge, but in the field of the courage needed for action. We all find it easier to know what to do rather than to actually do it.

It may be a situation in which selfish birth control is a powerfully attractive answer, and more than human courage is needed to avoid choosing it. Perhaps you may have taken a false stand and need extra courage to tell your partner that you are wrong. Maybe a child needs discipline and you are afraid to give it. There are so many situations in daily life when an added burst of courage is required. Sometimes, apparently out of the blue, you will feel this added push to take the step that should be taken. This push comes from the sacramental grace of Matrimony.

Live the Sacrament of Matrimony

Your task is to live the sacrament of Matrimony because everything you do as a husband or wife, father or mother really is part of the sacrament. The sacrament really just begins on your marriage day. As the union between Christ and his Church is a permanent one, so is the union between husband and wife. St. Robert Bellarmine tells us that in a certain sense we can compare marriage to the Blessed Sacrament itself. When the priest cradles in his hands the wafer of bread, he pronounces the sacramental words only once, but the sacrament itself, the presence of Christ, remains as long as the appearances of bread remain. In the same way you speak the sacramental words of your marriage vows only once but the sacrament itself remains.

As you leave the sanctuary arm in arm you will be a new husband and wife about to begin the great adventure of living the sacrament of Matrimony in all its depths and joys. Your whole married life is sacramentalized. Just as a person's whole life is changed by the reception of Holy Orders, so your life will be made different by Matrimony. When a priest preaches, teaches, celebrates Mass, visits the sick, he is fulfilling the role given him by Holy Orders. In a similar way when you perform the various duties toward each other and toward your children you will be living the sacrament of Matrimony. This means that every act of love, great or small, for each other or for the children is sacramental and increases sanctifying grace in your soul. These acts are not merely good works but sacramentalized works.

This sacramental love covers everything in married love. Whatever each one does becomes a living of the sacrament of Matrimony. Whether one or both work outside the home, whether they mow the lawn, do the household chores, nurse minor ailments, or soothe bruised feelings — all are part of living the sacrament of Matrimony.

Cooperation

Christ will come to you on your wedding day. He will remain with you and he will bring special helps. But you must use these graces. God helps those who help themselves is so true. Listen to what Pius XII told a group of newlyweds: ''It is a law of divine providence in the supernatural order that men do not reap the full fruit of the sacraments which they receive . . . unless they cooperate with grace. The grace of Matrimony will remain for the most part an unused talent, hidden in the field unless the parties exercise the supernatural powers and cultivate and develop the seeds of grace they have received. If, however, doing all that lies within their power, they cooperate diligently, they will be able with ease to bear the burdens of their state and to fulfill their duties. By such a sacrament they will be strengthened, sanctified, and in a manner consecrated.''

PART 2
WHO YOU ARE

personality
background
sexual differences

chapter 4
personality

Our first three chapters presented some fundamental ideas about marriage as a vocation, the purposes of marriage, and marriage as a sacrament.

These next three chapters will consider some basic facts about you and your partner as the individuals who will unite in marriage. Two different personalities of different sexes and from different backgrounds must unite to become one. "Henceforth you belong entirely to each other; you will be one in mind, one in heart, and one in affection." These words stress the unity that is so necessary in married life.

This need for unity calls for a great deal of understanding of self and the other plus great efforts to work at an ideal marriage unity.

You Are Different

It is very important to realize that each individual is unique. In the literal sense of the phrase God threw the mold away when he made each individual. You differ from everyone else because you share in a special way in the perfection and goodness of God. Your body differs from every other human body because it was made for your soul; your soul, also, differs from every other human soul precisely because it was created to give life to your body. You are neither body nor soul but both joined in the unity of your own person. Soul and body are made to work together in mutual harmony with each other.

The Mystery of Self

Each individual is a mystery not fully knowable even by himself. This surely is advantageous in the sense that a man and woman cannot become bored as they uncover more and more of the mystery of the other. There is always more to know and to love.

You must respect the individuality of the other and not try to change each other according to your own standard. A person who tries to change the other feels that there is only one way of looking at a situation, only one way of acting or reacting, and that happens to be his way. This is a very narrow viewpoint that effectively blocks communication and union. You must leave your partner in his or her "otherness." Each is a person before he is a spouse. Even after marriage each one must remain a person with his own dignity and rights. A marriage partner should not become a carbon copy of the other but must remain true to his/her own nature and identity. There will always be some points on which you will not see eye to eye with your partner. Accept and don't try to change.

Remember the story of the old Quaker who said to his wife, "Everybody in the world is odd except thee and me and I begin to wonder about thee at times." To make yourself the standard of all excellence is the height of conceit. To expect your partner to be, think, and act as you do is unrealistic, unloving, and productive of unhappiness.

Temperament

There are many ancient and modern terms used to explain basic differences in people. Based on temperament — and our understanding of it — each one of us has different psychological traits.

What is a temperament? It is an inborn tendency to certain special forms of behavior. Thus one has an inborn tendency to see the bright side of life and be cheerful, while another has an inclination to see the gloomy side of life and be sad.

Your temperament is merely a part of your personality. It is a tendency to certain modes of acting, but only a tendency not a necessity. Each temperament has good and bad inclinations, the good to be developed, the bad to be controlled. It might help you to realize that often a person's good quality when carried to excess becomes his bad quality. Thus a person may be an easygoing individual who does not hurt anyone, but he may be so easygoing that he may neglect the good he should do or allow the evil that he should prevent.

Character is what you do with your temperament, training, and environment. You are not responsible for your temperament but you are for your character. God gives you your free will and his grace, the necessary helps to develop a good character.

Here are four types of temperament.

First Type

This type of person is a forceful character with strong drives and emotions. He has powerful drives for food, sex, luxury, leadership. He is ambitious and sees opportunities as well as dangers.

His difficulty is that he drives himself too hard. He is the "ulcer type," who can give ulcers to himself and others. In his efforts to reach his goal he often does not even notice the needs and feelings of others. If others stand in the way of his goals, he has a tendency to walk over them. He is a great competitor and will push himself on to success in anything he tackles.

In marriage a man of this type may drive himself so hard in his business that he has no time for his wife and family. He feels that he is a good husband and father by providing a good standard of living for his family. A woman of this type may dominate her husband and will tend to nag and be bossy.

Confidence or trust in themselves comes easily to such men and women. Humility, sympathy, and forgiveness come with difficulty.

Second Type

This type of person is happy, warm, cheerful, outgoing. His emotions sparkle but do not burn deeply. He can become very excited but lose his interest quickly. A gift is received with a great manifestation of gratitude which can be easily forgotten. Such a person is optimistic and reacts greatly to praise and honors.

On the negative side this type is very restless and not a good sitter. He can be very curious and can turn into a busybody. Good times and parties are very enjoyable to him. But he may not wear too well over the long haul. Self-examination and introspection are avoided as much as possible. He feels that time will take care of problems. At times he can be very flighty and irresponsible.

There is no need to stress the importance of responsibility in marriage. A sanguine husband can be a floater who drifts from one job to another. He can leave the care of the children completely to the mother. He can be a very good salesman because he likes to meet people. A sanguine wife may be a very poor housekeeper who is more interested in going than staying. She may be unable to spend money wisely.

Third Type

This type of person is very ingoing, an introvert who finds himself more at home in his own internal world than in the external world of people and things. His emotions are deep and powerful. He is very sensitive and his feelings can be hurt very easily. He loves and hates intensely; he is a good friend and a bad enemy. Others find it difficult to communicate with him because he does not like others to know him from the inside. Pessimism comes readily to him. Sometimes such a person is the great reformer who seldom smiles and doggedly pursues his course. Many great teachers, poets, and artists have this kind of temperament.

A husband or wife of this type is very difficult to live with because he/she is subject to moods which start and stop without any reason apparent to the partner. The moody person pulls into his shell and will not let the partner follow. Such an individual finds it difficult to live with himself and others. A person married to this type often just gives up in disgust and goes his own way because he does not know how to cope with the various moods. No one can be the same at all times, as each one has different moods. But when moods are too deep, too frequent, and too lasting there is real trouble not only for the moody one but for the whole family.

Fourth Type

This type of person is usually easygoing with neither a great show of emotions or a deep intensity of them. He does not go up or down too much but keeps on a rather even line. He is ordinarily in calm possession of himself and is not easily disturbed. He usually has good judgment but not too much push to action. He seems to be without fire in his decisions, emotions, and actions. But he does have a great quality of stick-to-it-iveness and does get there.

No one possesses one temperament exclusively; each individual has a mixture of several temperaments with usually one predominating.

A husband and wife of different temperaments easily complement each other and fit together. The fourth type will calm down the first type, while the first will stimulate the fourth. The second can help brighten the life of a third. A third type husband and wife would have trouble communicating and have a very dark view of life. The union between people of the first type would be explosive. Two of the fourth type would get along but not get much done. Two of the second type would have trouble with living up to their responsibilities.

Accept your own temperament and the temperament of your partner. Work with your good as well as with your bad qualities. Understand your partner and help each other gradually to develop good qualities and control the bad ones. Do not blame your bad actions on your temperament, but on your character which has not controlled the bad inclinations of your temperament. You cannot justify your actions by appealing to your temperament because character must direct temperament. True understanding of self and the other leads to a very happy marriage.

Human Needs

Another way to look at yourselves as individual persons united as one in marriage is to examine your human needs and plan to fulfill them in each other. Abraham H. Maslow, a highly respected psychologist, explains his theory of human needs in his book *Motivation and Personality*. The following pages — presented as an aid to marriage partners — briefly explain his theory.

Human beings the world over have a common set of needs. We are born with them. Our thoughts and actions are all organized around them. Only when they are met can we experience happiness.

These needs do not demand satisfaction all at once. They are an orderly group. Each appears in its turn. Rarely do more than two demand our attention at one time.

Seven Basic Human Needs

There are seven basic human needs. Imagine them occupying the rungs of a ladder. Each need must be satisfied in order, the lower first and then the higher. A higher need lies dormant and is of no concern to us until the need immediately below is met.

7) **Beauty**

6) **Knowledge**

5) **Self-expression**

4) **Esteem**

3) **Love & Belonging**

2) **Safety**

1) **Body Needs**

(1) *Body Needs:*

First we must be fed, clothed, and sheltered. The needs of the body are on the lowest rung of the ladder. They must be satisfied (at least partially, as the ascetics did) before our thoughts can turn to higher things.

(2) *Safety:*

After the body is provided for we concern ourselves with safety. No man can function under an ever-present cloud of danger. Freedom from threat and injury are so necessary that we will sacrifice money, comfort, even dignity simply to be safe.

Body and safety needs are very strong. In emergencies they cause us to act in ways that later embarrass and shame us. Fortunately they are the easiest to satisfy. A simple but balanced diet, covering against the elements, protection against immediate attack is basically sufficient. Anything more elaborate is a luxury, not a necessity.

(3) *Love and Belonging:*

We all have a strong need to be affectionate and to belong to a group. Even the man leading a solitary life in the back reaches of Alaska carries with him the warm memory of a mother, a wife, or a friend. Both giving and receiving love are necessary. The person who takes love but does not give in return is meeting his need but not the need of the other.

(4) *Esteem:*

Esteem reaches beyond the confines of love. Love is a gift freely exchanged; there are no conditions. Beyond this we need to feel competent, to do something well. We need recognition, or esteem, from our fellow-man that says, "Good work, we need you." At the very least there must be an internal recognition that we are useful.

(5) *Self-expression:*

A clear human need exists to develop our personal abilities, to use our talents, to choose for ourselves what we will become. Self-expression is the key to a person's individuality. We may have a well-paying job and our skill is fully appreciated; but because we are not expressing what is unique to ourselves we are unhappy. Under these circumstances only a change of jobs or outside activity that allows us to express our interests will fulfill this need.

(6) *Knowledge:*

We all have a built-in curiosity. As children we constantly ask questions and are forever exploring the world about us. We never outgrow this need. As adults our world expands to include everything from atoms to zeppelins. We always remain children in our uncomplicated need to investigate the mysterious — to know.

(7) *Beauty:*

There must be some beauty in our lives. We cannot tolerate perpetual ugliness. Many find enjoyment in one of the art forms: dancing, reading, sculpting, painting. Others find it in the more physical aspects of the world that surrounds us. Human tastes range widely in meeting this need.

Ability to Satisfy Basic Needs

We all have the ability to satisfy these seven basic needs. As one level is satisfied the next higher emerges. No one has to teach us what comes next. It springs into the open under its own power. We thus grow from within like a blossoming flower. That is our human nature.

To achieve happiness we must attend to our real wants. We must ignore the pressures to eat more food, wear fancier clothes, buy newer cars. Those things will not satisfy us adequately. We must look to what we genuinely crave. What basic human need is going unsatisfied? Answering that question requires an honest look at ourselves. Some may need the help of another person in order to see more clearly. Always the answer lies within the individual person.

We human beings often do not develop to our full potential. We get stuck at one need level; we are frustrated. Usually we are trying to satisfy a need in an inefficient way. Consider the person who continually feels unsafe. He reacts to every situation as a threat to himself. He is wary, suspicious, building walls against imaginary dangers. He cannot think of love or beauty. His physical and mental energies are directed toward making his world safe. As others pull away from him he feels more threatened and grows ever more suspicious. (Often, behind the fashionable wardrobe and the sleek automobile is a very unhappy person.)

Everyone can learn new ways to fill a need. The insecure person mentioned above may well be suffering from early traumatic experiences. He may still be living in a world where he was indeed unsafe. With the help of professionals and a great deal of personal effort, he can learn to live in the present world. Overcoming these fears he emerges a new person. More correctly he becomes truly himself, capable now of loving and giving expression to the higher human needs. No matter how bleak the picture, we all have the capacity to change for the better.

Your Marriage

People marry because they love each other. That is no profound secret. Two people are attracted to one another for satisfaction of their need to give and to receive love.

But love alone is not enough. A marriage must foster growth at all levels. It must be beyond love and satisfy the partners in their need for esteem, self-expression, knowledge, and beauty.

Marriage is not the conclusion of a ceremony. It is a lifelong task in which both partners help each other to grow as perfect and fulfilled as possible. It begins with love and matures to include all human needs.

Marriages fail because the partners are frustrated in their higher needs, not because love has died. Human beings need more than love to be happy. "I love you, but . . ." is the refrain of every poor marriage.

Beyond Love

After love there are four levels of human need. Tack

the short list below to your mental bulletin board and refer to it often.

BEAUTY
KNOWLEDGE
SELF-EXPRESSION
ESTEEM

These four steps are rungs 7, 6, 5, and 4 of the human need ladder. When problems and conflicts occur in your marriage, ask yourself the simple question, "What need is my partner trying to meet and how can I help?"

Here are a few ideas on just how to put these steps into practice.

Esteem: (Step 4)

Needs do not discriminate between the sexes. Husband, remember that your wife must feel competent at a job and receive recognition for her skill. Encourage her efforts and don't be afraid to say, "That looks good."

Wife, your husband needs understanding when his job goes poorly, when his self-esteem hits bottom. Let his irritable remarks pass harmlessly by. Help him to find a better way to approach his job. Be enthusiastic. Trust in his abilities. Be proud of him.

Self-expression: (Step 5)

Both marriage partners need an activity that develops their individual abilities. This need has been largely overlooked for women. A wife has the need to choose for herself the direction she will go — a job outside the home, volunteer work, perhaps continuing her education.

Husband, give your wife the emotional freedom to choose. Respect her interests. Share in the household tasks. Do not begrudge the time she is away.

Wife, does your husband enjoy his work? Does he find it fulfilling? If he must change jobs, suffer through the uncertainty with him. Don't be jealous of a hobby that relieves his frustrations. Be glad of his independence; share in his accomplishments.

Knowledge: (Step 6)

What does your spouse enjoy learning about? Develop new common interests. Keep your minds alive and you will never grow bored with one another or with yourself.

Beauty: (Step 7)

In what does your spouse see beauty? A symphony, a well-built house, a flawlessly executed football play? There is harmony and balance in anything done well. Do not close your mind to the things that give your spouse enjoyment. Learn to see the beauty there and you will grow closer to one another.

Living with Your Human Needs

You behave in certain ways in order to meet your most pressing need. Not all of your married life will be spent seeking knowledge and beauty. Money, your relationship with your in-laws, shoes for the children, pressures from outside the home — all these will make demands upon your time and energy. Do not be surprised when, at the end of a long and exhausting day, you cannot muster feelings of affection and esteem for your mate. You need rest, time alone, a little food. Likewise, don't expect too much from your partner. Allow the lower needs to be filled before looking for the more noble.

Above all, do not ignore or be ashamed of your human needs. They are an intimate part of you. Use them as a clear map to personal happiness. Make room in your life and your marriage for the higher needs that go beyond love. They are a necessary part of your life. Your marriage can starve from lack of esteem; it can wither without self-expression. It will grow boring without common interests; it will lack harmony without beauty.

Marriage adds to your capacity to be fully satisfied at all levels of your life. It takes nothing away. Enter and live your marriage with the confident thought that while the demands are many, great are the rewards.

chapter 5
background

You must realize that you and your partner have a different heredity and come from different backgrounds. Marriage calls for a great deal of understanding so that you can become one despite these differences.

You and your mate will not appear out of nowhere and meet at the altar. You bring your family, friends, education, and all the many factors that helped form you. Heredity and environment have exercised a great influence on you. It is very difficult to distinguish the precise influence of each of these two factors on any individual. This is not very important for our purpose as we are not writing a scientific treatise but a practical guide to help you know and love the other. If you are to live with another person for life, you should know a great deal about the various factors that formed your partner's character. This chapter will call your attention to some of the basic influences that should be known before marriage.

Home

You learn much about your future companion when you see him in his home. The most important quality in the home is the love that unites all the members into a happy family. In the closeness of family life a person is training for his own life and his own family. In his home he learns how to give and receive love, how to respect others, how to carry his share of the burdens of family life, to rejoice in the good things, and not fall apart in trials and tribulations. These and so many other good qualities are learned, sometimes unconsciously, by training and example in the home. It is difficult to substitute for the influence of a good home. You can judge how your partner will treat you when you see how he treats his parents, his brothers and sisters, and his friends. A person does not change radically so that he treats his own family poorly and after marriage changes completely and treats you well. People do not change overnight. His actions in his parents' home will be a good indication of his future actions in his own home.

Love and the ability to give of self are necessary in marriage. You can learn whether your future partner is capable of showing love by his conduct in his home. Sometimes one who is born in a family that does not show affection finds it extremely difficult to show love in his own marriage. A child must not only know that he is loved and that things such as food and clothing are given out of love. But he must emotionally feel that he is loved and appreciated as a person. Physical and verbal expressions of love make a child realize he is truly loved. One who does not know how to give and receive love can be an emotional cripple in marriage.

A sense of security, a feeling of self-confidence, is needed by every mature person and only a mature person is capable of accepting the responsibilities of marriage. A person must feel needed and wanted. This sense of belonging comes from his own incorporation into his family life. The person who does not feel that he belongs is always trying to prove that he does belong and is always looking for possible indications in the other to show that the other does not really need and want him. This can lead to many, many difficulties in married life. This need and want must be present on an emotional level. It is not enough to know in your mind but you must feel in your heart that you are needed and wanted. This feeling comes from the home.

The sense of cooperation, the feeling that all are working together, talking together, laughing together, is also of great value in the home. A person who does not fit easily into the home pattern and is a loner will carry this same quality into marriage. Those about to marry must fully realize that marriage demands that a husband and wife work together to make their marriage a successful one. It is too big a task for one person alone! Two loners will never meet and work together. Each will go his separate way to the great harm of the marriage.

The true strength of a family is seen when sorrow comes. Whether it is death, mental illness, financial loss, or some other serious problem, the true mettle of the family is shown in the way they bear this cross. If they cannot face the problem and pull into their shells, or if they go to pieces, this is the way your future partner will probably act when trials appear. Sorrow and trials will be found in marriage and must be faced and settled or accepted according to circumstances. At such a time emotional control does not mean the suppression of emotions but a reasonable expression of the safety valves God has given human beings. Bottled-up emotions lead to much trouble.

A sense of humor, the ability to laugh at oneself as well as the other, makes life more enjoyable and livable. It is not good to take oneself too seriously. A partner from a family where laughter is found is a good matrimonial risk. Even serious matters such as religion, love, sex can have their lighter side.

Money

You should know your partner's attitude toward money. The financial condition of a family as well as its feelings toward money have an influence upon the members of the family. Your partner can come from a different financial level than you. This can lead to difficulties that should be faced before marriage. A person from a family that had to skimp to make ends meet might be very tight with money, or go the opposite extreme of spending it foolishly when some comes into his hands. One whose every whim has been satisfied by rich and indulgent parents will have no appreciation of the true value of money. He who has been indulged becomes very self-centered with no room in himself for thoughts about the other. Listen to how your partner and his family talk about money. This as well as the way they use it will reveal the value they place upon money. One who has had to work during his education or had to live within a strict budget will have a greater regard for money and use it wisely.

Education

The education of the man and woman can play a great role in the marriage. People with the same intellectual background have common interests and can more easily communicate. It is true that one without the same opportunities for formal education as the partner can be self-educated to his/her level or beyond it. A husband and wife with the same intellectual interests have a better chance for a happy marriage.

Health and Habits

The kind of health each person has will influence marriage greatly. A strong person who has never been sick a day in his life will expect more of himself and others. While the person who has been sickly can understand sickness but possibly can be given to self-pity. This difference can make it hard for each to understand the other.

You should also know your partner's living habits to see if you can live with him. There are night people and day people and it is not very easy for them to meet. The day person is the one who is up early, starts early, and finishes early in the day. The night person is up late, goes into action only late in the day, and continues late into the night. The difference between night people and day people can be a result of an overactive or underactive thyroid.

Men and women are regulated by their glands. A woman's menstrual cycle has a great influence on her mood at the time of ovulation and menstruation. Also the menopause or the stopping of the menstrual cycle can be a very emotional time in the woman. A woman's attitude toward these monthly events can have a great bearing on her happiness and that of her family. While men do not go through a definite cycle, yet at a somewhat later time in their life they go through a period that might be called "menablues." At such a time a man can become very worried and fearful of death, cancer, insanity, loss of manhood, and so forth. Also during this time usually his responsibilities toward the education of the children are greater and he begins to fear that he is not able to meet them. This, too, like the monthly cycle of the woman and the menopause, can be handled with tact and care.

Friends

There is an old axiom: "Tell me who your friends are and I will tell you what you are." This is so true, as friends are freely chosen while relatives are accepted of necessity. The type of friends shows one's values and preferences. It is, for instance, difficult for a non-drinker or moderate drinker to move with a fast-drinking crowd. Or again a person who delights in dirty stories will seek his own level of enjoyment. Take notice of how your intended partner relates with a small group or a large one. See whether he makes friends easily and loses them just as easily, or whether he keeps the friends he has made. You will learn how large a circle of friends he has and how close he is to them.

During courtship do not neglect your friends. You must grow and if you and your partner are always together and never with anyone else you will become bored with each other. Each individual has a certain amount to offer and personal growth demands contacts with others. You must grow so that you have more to offer each other. Don't lose your friends during courtship, as you need them then and will need them during your marriage. Try to become friends with your partner's friends, but keep at least some of your own friends even if your partner does not care for them.

Religion

Religious beliefs and practices before marriage are a good indication of the place religion will hold in your marriage. One who believes and follows his religious convictions should continue to do so after marriage. A lax person will not normally change unless some conversion takes place through his own efforts or that of his partner. It sometimes happens that a young person goes through a period of rebellion against the restraints of religion. But this can be a passing phase that will not prevent a return to religion with maturity. Religion should be openly discussed before marriage. If there is a difference in religious beliefs, you and your partner should agree on a program of action. All things being equal, a husband and wife who agree on basic religious matters will pull together better as a team.

Influence of Home

You may have a negative reaction to something you did not like in your family's home, and you are determined it will not happen in your home. A girl whose father is an alcoholic will be very sensitive to anything approaching a drinking problem. A man whose mother never showed any affection to his father will be very certain that his wife will show affection to him. If the husband comes from a home where his mother has dominated his father he is definite that this will not happen in his home. But if the wife comes from a home where her father dominated her mother she, too, enters with the idea that this will not happen. Both will enter marriage with the idea that the other is not going to dominate. This can only lead to tragedy.

Conscious Carry-over

A person's background may carry over into his marriage in different ways. In a very conscious way he may determine to definitely bring some good things to his marriage and just as definitely to keep others out of his marriage. He will want the good things of his parents' marriage to be in his marriage. It may be something important, such as religious beliefs and practices, an open display of affection, or a spirit of friendliness and cooperation. It may be something small as the arrangement of meals on Sunday.

There are also many unconscious attitudes that you will bring into marriage. Since you are not even aware that these attitudes exist and are busy at work below the conscious level, they will have a great influence on you and your marriage. Sometimes a marriage counselor is needed to uncover these unconscious feelings which are harming a marriage.

Love and understanding will help you in the lifelong adjustment to each other.

chapter 6
sexual differences

The third bridge that must be crossed before you or your partner can become one is the difference between the sexes. You and your husband share the same common human nature but with some important variations.

Many tests confirm great similarities between the sexes but also point out differences. Some of these variations come from the biological function of each sex; others arise from training and education; others from the roles assigned to the sexes by our culture.

In this chapter we will try to outline in a rather black and white fashion some of the important characteristics of each sex. But it is well to realize that each sex has both masculine and feminine qualities. The more normal a person is the more he balances in himself the good qualities of both sexes. Human nature is both male and female and the more human one becomes the more he unites both sides of human nature in himself. Also each sex finds itself through a good relationship with the opposite sex. A man becomes more masculine and a woman becomes more feminine in a mature relationship with each other. Each sex learns from the other. Education, also, helps to develop a better-balanced human personality.

Without even fully realizing it each sex can feel that the other sex thinks, feels, and acts in the same way as it does. A wife may say: "If I love someone I would not treat her like my husband treats me." Or a husband may complain: "What is she so worried about? Surely I love her." All that either can logically conclude is that if I as a man or a woman said or did something it would mean this to me. It is illogical and unreasonable to go beyond this and say therefore it must mean the same to the other. The realization of this truth makes understanding easier and communication better.

A better understanding of the differences between the sexes will prevent you from judging matters between yourselves in too personal a way.

The tendency is to say: "It is my husband or my wife who is acting in this way and causing all the trouble." Often the true situation should be stated: "It is a husband and a wife acting like husbands and wives do act." When words and actions are seen in this wider frame of reference they are much easier to understand and handle. This knowledge takes the personal sting out of many problems and makes them problems common to many husbands and wives.

Basic Roles

A man and a woman cannot be understood apart from the basic roles which God prepared them to fulfill. A man is prepared for fatherhood and a woman for motherhood. The purpose for which God destined man and woman determines the way in which he made them physically and psychologically.

As long ago as the 13th century, St. Thomas held that man by nature is meant to be father, protector, and provider. This fact of potential fatherhood explains the physical, psychological, and spiritual characteristics of man.

Woman is biologically and psychologically prepared for motherhood. This idea has been well expressed by Pope Pius XII in an address to Catholic women: "Every woman is made to be a mother in the physical sense of the word, or indeed in the more spiritually exalted but no less real sense. To this end the Creator ordained a whole characteristic constitution of woman, her organic make-up and even more her spirit and above all her delicate sensitiveness.'' Motherhood is woman's destiny and the religious nun and single woman must attain spiritual motherhood if they are to be fulfilled as women.

Physical Differences

In general a man's body is stronger than a woman's. He was made to be provider and protector of the family and for this reason has been given greater strength. Science and experience point out that a woman's body can endure pain better than a man's, but a man's body is more capable of hard physical labor.

It is obvious that a woman's whole physical constitution is destined for the conception, caring, delivery, and nursing of the child. Her grace and beauty — of body, mind, and heart — attract man's interest and lead to a better knowledge and love which in turn lead to marriage.

Sense Knowledge

Knowledge is very important. It enables people to be in contact with the outside world and to respond to it in a meaningful way. All human beings are capable of two kinds of knowledge: sense knowledge and intellectual knowledge. By sense knowledge is meant knowledge of material things — things that can be seen, heard, smelled, tasted, and felt, as well as the imagination and memories of these material objects. Most of these ways of knowing are not fully appreciated. It is usually only when one is faced with a malfunction or a deprivation of one of the senses that its true value is recognized.

How do men and women differ with regard to sense knowledge? Sometimes it is said that one of the most typically feminine characteristics is the ability to observe details. Does this mean that a woman's senses are keener than a man's? Can she see smaller details, hear finer distinctions in sounds, etc? No. All the evidence states that there is no superior sex with regard to the functioning of the senses. Besides, that is not what is meant when it is stated that women are more observant of details. What is really meant is that they are more interested in details than men. So what is implied is that men cannot be bothered. Supposedly, they have the big issues of life to be concerned with and cannot be bothered with minutiae.

To demonstrate this point usually an example such as this is brought up: After a party attended by both the husband and the wife, ask each of them separately what he or she observed: "Who was there? What clothes did they wear? What was the color of the wallpaper? How was the furniture arranged? What did each person say?" To most of these questions the man will be able to give only the vaguest answers. He really did not notice most of these things. He could have if he had wanted to, but he did not. But the wife was interested in these things and she could get on the phone and spend an hour describing each and every detail of the party to one of her women friends.

The above example would probably turn out as described. Still, the proposed distinction comes across as oversimplified: that women are great on details and men are not because they are occupied with the big picture.

First of all, the broadly educated, well-informed alert woman of today is just as capable as any man of having worthwhile opinions on practically any major subject being currently discussed. She might have trouble finding someone to listen to her seriously; but this is obviously a prejudice of society and society's loss. And with regard to men, is it really true that they cannot handle details. Is it true that they will not get interested in details? Take a look inside the cockpit of a 747. Ask a research scientist or a computer programmer if details are unimportant. Inquire of a lawyer if it is necessary to read the fine print. The working lives of many men are nothing but details day in and day out. The men are not

49

only handling these details competently but they seem to be interested in them.

Different Approach

Nonetheless, it must be admitted that there is a difference in the way that men and women approach details. Is it that men are concerned with important details and women with unimportant ones? It depends on what a person considers to be important. Are the many small duties of a housewife and mother unimportant — cooking the meals, mending the clothes, shopping, cleaning the house, getting the children off to school, etc.? Is it of no importance that a mother would stop what she is doing to answer a child's question or pay attention to what has been discovered in play? A recent three-year study by a team of Harvard researchers came up with the conclusion that "mothering is a highly underrated profession." How the mother does her job, the skill she brings to it, especially in the early years, is critically important in determining the child's positive self-image, his/her competence in learning, and his/her future character development. Once again to really understand men and women there has to be a frequent return to the basic God-given roles of fatherhood and motherhood.

Looking at it from that viewpoint, then, it can be seen that a man's skill zeros in on those details which make him a better provider-protector — usually those details connected with his work or some of the heavier maintenance jobs of his home. A woman focuses on the so-called "little things" that nourish and strengthen the inner life of the family. But both men and women have shown themselves capable of facing the big questions of life. It is true that a man's working day might bring him more contacts with what are thought of as these larger questions of life (business matters involving a lot of money, politics, national security, international problems of energy, environmental questions, threats of war, etc.).

On the other hand, the wife has spent her day in the

Lilliputian world of children. (But, lest we forget, these little ones are going to grow up some day. They are going to have to run this troubled world. Will they be equipped for it? Will they be properly formed?) Whatever the future holds, at the present moment the mother is confined all day to the four walls of a rather limited child-size universe. No wonder that she is so hungry for her husband by the time he arrives home. She is so ready to talk to him on her own adult level that she might not let him get a word in edgewise.

It is good for both sexes to realize these differences. Especially crucial are the first minutes of their meeting at the end of the workday. Their heads will be so filled with their own worlds that it might be very difficult to have a meeting of the minds. Probably the only way will be by first having a meeting of their hearts. The love each has will urge them to try to learn and understand more and more about the other's working world.

Sometimes it happens that a husband can get a convincing introduction into this world of his spouse when she has to be away for a few days. It usually turns out to be a baptism of fire. ''Running the house'' for even such a short time is enough to drive the ordinary man almost out of his mind. And when the wife returns, she will probably have to spend several more days to get everything working smoothly again.

The Emotions

Sense knowledge brings about favorable or unfavorable reactions. These motions toward the good and pleasant objects and away from the bad and unpleasant ones are called emotions. These emotions can be divided into two groups: (1) the pure-and-simple emotions and (2) the facing-a-challenge emotions.

The first group, the pure-and-simple emotions, includes love, hate, desire, aversion, joy, and sorrow. These belong together because each is a pure-and-simple movement toward or away from an object or a person. It is all clear-cut and unambiguous. They single-mindedly focus on the object, and that becomes the whole world for the present moment. So, although they are pure-and-simple, they can pervade someone's whole personality and become extremely strong. In fact, any one of these emotions can be so powerful and all-encompassing as to determine the entire thrust of a person's life. There is a saying that "love makes the world go round," and it contains a lot of truth. The other emotions in this group can be equally strong in their motivating force.

The second group, the facing-a-challenge emotions, includes anger, daring, hope, fear, and despair. Each one of these has to do with the presence of an obstacle, something blocking the way, something keeping a person from reaching a desired good or avoiding a threatening evil. These are sometimes called the "emergency emotions." There comes to mind the rapid heartbeat, the quick breathing, the muscle-tensing of an adrenalin-spiked system. All are part of the picture of anger, fear, etc. Needless to say, these emotions can be very strong. In fact, they can and frequently do lead to violent behavior.

Clearly, a man or a woman — either one, equally — can be moved by any of the above emotions from either grouping. Surely there have been men motivated by love, hate, etc. Women, too, have been known to get angry on occasion. "Hell hath no fury like a woman scorned." Usually, however, women are said to be inclined more toward the first group, and men toward the second group. Is there something about their life styles or work patterns that have tilted the different sexes in one direction or another?

A man might have to spend a large part of his day in what could be a very hostile world. Recent research on work, and what most people think of it, seems to verify this. For many working people it is a daily struggle — an eight-to-five battle. If the husband has had such a day, and if he has to fight traffic on the way home, it is not surprising if he arrives there in a belligerent mood. He is bound to find it hard not to carry over some of his aroused aggressive emotions into the gentler environment of his home. In turn, his wife and children, not sufficiently aware of what he has gone through, would probably interpret these emotions as directed toward themselves. So a new strain is placed upon the harmony and peace of the family.

One of the most frequent complaints lodged against husbands by wives is that men are obstinate. It is true that they often are, and sometimes unreasonably so, but if a man did not have a pretty stiff backbone he would not be able to provide much support and protection for his family against the assaults of a threatening world. Again, it is part of his basic role as protector and provider. Sometimes what looks like obstinancy and stubbornness really turns out to be determination or perseverance in working toward a goal — certainly traits that a man needs.

Normally, when a man acquires a family he sets many goals for himself. He dreams many dreams. There are many things he wants to do for his family. But these dreams do not materialize so easily in the daylight of this highly competitive world. It takes a lot of hard work and there are frequent frustrations. When difficult times come, self-doubts and misgivings can also come. He wonders whether he is doing well enough in his work, whether there is enough future in his job, so that he will always be able to give his family the things he wants them to have. He has doubts about whether he is spending too much time making a living and not enough time truly "living" with his wife and children. He is providing his family with the necessities of life and even some of the lesser luxuries. But is he giving enough of himself, his presence, his companionship?

Different Aspects

There are so many aspects in which a man may doubt himself in his role of protector-provider that he needs the constant encouragement and assurance of his wife. Because of her affectionate, warm, person-centered nature she is especially equipped to provide him with this needed solace. She must make him realize that she is back of him all the way. She must show that she is satisfied with the work he is doing, as well as the way he supports the family. She should never belittle. Since she knows him so well, she could attack him on his weakest points. Spouses are always very vulnerable to each other. Such an attack can completely demoralize him. Rather than tear down, she should help him build up his self-confidence. He has to be assured of his own adequacy and importance if he is to continue to function as father of the family.

This is a very fundamental point and is the reason why so much is written about the evil of nagging. To nag means "to annoy by continual faultfinding, complaining, and urging." Besides the harm it does to the morale of the husband, it does not accomplish its purpose, which is to force him to ask for a raise, to stand up to someone at work, to push forward, etc. The nagging does not work because it is missing its target. It implies bad will, sloth, or irresponsibility, and does not recognize the real reason why a man is failing to do something. That buried reason can only be unearthed if the couple learns how to communicate. That means listening to and understanding each other's deeper feelings. Nagging is the opposite of such respectful communication. It chips away at a man's pride and undermines his self-image. And in doing this to her husband, she is also doing herself in. A woman can never destroy a man's pride and still retain his love.

A woman's emotions, whether of the pure-and-simple type or the facing-a-challenge type, are closer to the surface than a man's. They are ready to bubble over quite easily. Usually she can express her feelings more readily. Her heart is easily moved. She is quick to sympathize, perceptive of others, sensitive, and easily hurt.

It is important for a husband to realize that his wife is person-centered in her approach to everything. She is interested in persons, always and everywhere. Interpersonal relationships mean a great deal to her. She is especially personal in her own life; very likely she will take everything personally. As a consequence, a man can hurt her feelings without even realizing the reason why. Whatever is said, whatever is done is interpreted by her in this personal way. When this happens — and she is hurt, perhaps even to tears — it is no use for the man to argue logically that she has drawn the wrong conclusion from his words or actions. It would be far better if he took her in his arms and told her how wonderful she is. That would be meeting the situation where it really is.

What it comes down to is the paramount importance a woman places on her relationship with her spouse. This is all-important to her. Apparently she has sensed some threat to that. She will not be at peace until she has been reassured that nothing is changing that relationship. If she receives that assurance, if he can convince her of that, if he can show her that she is still the object of his love, as she always was, then the house can collapse about her and she will stand there in the rubble and be unafraid. Sure of her loved one's love, she will be courageous and confident and, in turn, a source of strength for her husband.

Intellectual Knowledge

There are differences in the way in which the male and female minds usually work. A man's mind is called logical; a woman's mind is referred to as intuitional. It is well to remember that neither sex always acts in this special way. Both approaches to truth are used at different times and under different circumstances by each sex.

A man normally approaches a problem by the slow and methodical method of analysis. He tries to take each step and figure it out carefully; he weighs the pros and the cons before making a decision. The good aspect of this method is that it is prudent and can prevent hasty mistakes; the bad side is that it can become over-cautious and be unable to make any decision because it sees too well the difficulties on both sides. A man can become so careful and want to be so sure before he makes a move that he does not make any moves at all.

As a result of this logical frame of mind a man's thinking is also compartmental. This means that a man sees various aspects of his life in a separate and not united fashion. His life is divided between his work, his family, his recreation, and so forth. It is therefore possible for these different facets of his life to compete with each other. Thus he can be torn between the attention he gives to his family and his work. Man works because he has to support his family. But he also works and pursues his hobbies because he likes to do so and finds fulfillment in them. A man must keep a balance between his work, his family, and his recreation.

Intuition

Intuition means to leap in a flash to the very heart of the matter. Often a woman cannot explain the steps which led her to a specific solution but she is absolutely convinced that she has made the right decision. Intuition, as it were, telescopes the steps and arrives quickly at the center of the truth. It is the ability of the mind to see things not so much in their parts but as a whole. Intuition at its best leads quickly and surely to the truth; at its worst it leads to rash and imprudent decisions.

In keeping with her intuitional approach to truth is a woman's approach toward life and marriage. She sees things as a whole and everything else in proper subordination to that whole. In marriage a woman considers everything in relationship to her husband and children. She does not divide things into compartments as readily as a man does. Because of the heritage of her basic role, her thoughts more likely would run along domestic lines. This is especially true if she does not work outside the home. She will have many interests, but her thoughts will center on her home and on her family. In such a friendly setting intuitional thinking could blossom. It could become the usual mode of her thoughts.

The logical and the intuitional approach to truth are complementary ways of arriving at truth. As in so many other ways, the husband and the wife can complete or complement each other. To rely entirely on the man's progressive form of reasoning would be to delay many decisions that should be made at once. On the other hand, to depend completely on a woman's intuitional procedure would lead to many rash decisions. The extreme of man's approach is inactivity; the extreme of woman's approach is impulsiveness. She can spur him on, while he can check her.

The husband and wife often find it difficult to understand each other's approach to life and marriage. A man can find it difficult to understand his wife's interests; a woman may find it very difficult to understand her man's interests. There must be mutual understanding and compromise in this field. When there is an unselfish love a solution will be found. A man must learn to bring his hobbies and recreation into proper relationship with his family life; the wife must learn to share some of them and willingly allow her husband to indulge in others on his own.

Realism and Idealism

His whole aggressive nature as father, protector, and provider leads man to realism. He is moved by the demands of practical life and sets very objective goals for himself. He is concerned about earning a living, providing a good home, taking care of the education of the children.

As a realist, man can often have real doubts about himself and his ability to provide for his family. Discouragement is a basic problem and therefore encouragement a basic need of a husband and father. A man may wonder whether he is doing well enough to support his family, whether there is enough future in his job so that he can give his family the things he wants them to have. He has doubts whether he is spending too much time in the making of a living and not enough time with his wife and children. He has misgivings about his relationship with his employers, his clients, or his employees. A man needs encouragement. This is why nagging is so destructive. It takes away his sense of pride and destroys his confidence in himself. The wife should always remember that she can never destroy a man's pride in himself and still retain his love. The husband by nature and by the acceptance of society is head of the home. The wife should recognize his role and his need and attempt not to dominate him but to win him over to her point of view by persuasion and diplomacy.

A woman is by her very nature idealistic in outlook. She is attracted by beauty and the grandeur of noble ideas. Her values are of a more romantic and idealistic sort. Her imagination and her heart are powerfully attuned to the beautiful. In her close contact with the children she can instill in them noble ideals and elevated standards.

A woman's basic need is for love and affection. She wants to be sought after, to be the chosen one, to be desired and loved. She craves for physical and verbal signs of love. She knows that she is loved but she wants to be told it many, many times. Often she will be forced to ask her husband: "Do you still love me?" To many men this is a foolish question because he feels that he proves his love by being at home, not running around, not drinking or gambling to excess and so forth. It is true that these are admirable qualities but the woman wants so much more than that. She wants not merely one who does not run around, drink or gamble to excess, and so forth, but she wants a person who loves her as a person. Too often men merely give things and not themselves to their wives. Things have value but the person is all-important to her. A man must notice his wife and praise her not only for what she does but for what she is. She *likes* it when he admires her style in clothes, but she *loves* it when he praises her personal accomplishments.

These are some of the basic ways in which men and women differ and yet complement each other. It takes great effort to fit in alongside each other yet it is a very rewarding experience. You can both learn from each other and grow into a well-balanced individual with the masculine and feminine traits in proper proportion.

PART 3
LIFE TOGETHER

love
talk and listen
the meaning of sex
anatomy
the art of love-making
responsible parenthood
your child
money
the working couple
relatives and friends
religion in your home

chapter 7
love

Once you know what marriage is and who you are you can look forward to your marriage. This last part of the book will explain some of the basic elements that make a happy and successful marriage.

Love

Love is one of the most used and least understood words in our language. People use the word very freely and it has a wide variety of meanings. "I love God," "I love you," "I love hot dogs." "I love you; therefore premarital sex is okay." "I no longer love you; therefore I divorce you."

In our society love leads to marriage. In other cultures partners are chosen by parents and love must begin and grow after marriage. But in our culture adults freely choose their partners and choose them usually out of love. Hence it is all-important that those about to marry understand the true nature of love.

Crush or Infatuation

Probably every boy and girl has suffered through a crush or infatuation. A girl may secretly adore the football star; a boy may nourish a hidden love for the school beauty. A young person has a great tendency to idealize persons without really knowing them. The idolized person occupies all the thoughts of the one with a crush. The word "infatuation" means to be foolish, to be without sound judgment. Truly a person thinks, dreams, and sometimes acts in a foolish way. This is a normal stage in the development of a mature relationship with the opposite sex. It is harmful only if it carries over into adult life or leads to a foolish marriage. This stage can be helpful because it makes the person become interested in the other sex and lets him realize that he can care for someone else.

Romantic Love

Romantic love is an emotional feeling that suddenly attracts a person to another without really knowing him. It is love at first sight. Usually it concentrates on surface qualities in the other, such as beauty, charm, or popularity. It is an unreal approach to love and life. A person who is in love with love is a romantic. Romantic love sees only peaks of love and is unaware of its valleys. It believes that love settles all. All romantic love ends with: "They married and lived happily ever after."

Marriage is not a romantic story but real life with sorrows as well as joys. Romantic love cannot weather storms because it does not even recognize their existence. If the partner does not measure up to the unrealistic standards, the marriage falls apart. True love really shows itself in difficulties. If the partner becomes entangled in a serious problem, the true lover will make every possible effort to help. When tragedy strikes a family a husband and wife are drawn closer together and see depths never before seen in each other. Sorrow unites those who love. There is no doubt that romance in the form of affection, tenderness, and consideration must be found in marriage. These qualities should be shown before marriage; and they are even more necessary after marriage to help love grow. Many a man and woman has been blinded by a great display of charm that vanishes afterward because it had no solid basis in the personality. Real love must wear well.

True Love

It is very difficult to define love, as the many and varied attempts show. There is so much involved that it is not easy to give a popular definition of love. Perhaps a good description of married love would be: "The gift of two people to each other in an exclusive and permanent union." Each person has a need to receive and a need to give.

Need to Receive

Every person is limited as a human being and as a particular human being. Each of us is incomplete and craves completion. As creatures we need our Creator for full completion; as men or women we need the other sex for human completion. This is what is meant in Genesis: "It is not good that the man is alone; I will make him a helper like himself" (Gn 2:18).

Thus a person is naturally attracted to one who has qualities that complement his. As was pointed out in an earlier chapter the sexes are different and they complete each other in many ways. The individual seeks out a person with the characteristics which blend with and strengthen his. Love looks for a loving and giving person with ideals and a sense of responsibility. These good qualities must be found in a pleasing personality. Otherwise, they will not lead to love.

Need to Give

Besides the need to receive there is also the need to give. True love is never content to merely receive. It is always moved to share what it has. This principle is clear in the mutual giving and loving of the Father, Son, and Holy Spirit in the intimate life of the Trinity. In creation God shared his perfections with all creatures and especially with man. God so loved the world that he gave his only Son for its redemption.

Man, who is made in the image and likeness of his Creator, shares, also, in this urge to give, to share with others what he has received. This desire to share comes from an unselfish love which cannot be content to keep everything for self. A good person naturally gives not only things such as money or toys, but gives self, his love, his time, his care, and concern.

Total Gift

He who loves gives himself completely in all ways, at

all times. He gives his affections so that the loved one occupies the central role in his life. He gives his body as an integral part of himself and as an expression of his love. He gives his thoughts, his attention, his considerateness to the other.

Love leads to the complete gift even to the point of sacrifice. This beautiful truth is found in the instruction that can be used in the marriage ceremony.

"It is most fitting that you rest the security of your wedded life upon the great principle of self-sacrifice. And so you begin your married life by the voluntary and complete surrender of your individual lives in the interest of that deeper and wider life which you are to have in common. Henceforth you belong entirely to each other; you will be one in mind, one in heart, and one in affection. And whatever sacrifices you may hereafter be required to make to preserve this common life, always make them generously. Sacrifice is usually difficult and irksome. Only love can make it easy; and perfect love can make it a joy. We are willing to give in proportion as we love. And when love is perfect, the sacrifice is complete. God so loved the world that he gave his only begotten Son, and the Son so loved us that he gave himself for our salvation. 'Greater love than this no man hath, that a man lay down his life for his friends.' "

Man in his incompleteness cries: "I need you"; in his creative love he proclaims: "I give you all." He also says: "I love you alone and I love you forever." This intimate, personal love is not given in the same way to any other person. He is faithful to the marriage vows made to his partner. This love is promised "in good times and in bad, in sickness and in health . . . all the days of my life." He loves in the sunshine as well as in the rain.

Practical Suggestions

1. *Love the other as a person.*

Your partner is a person to be loved and not a thing to be used for your selfish purposes. If you regard your partner merely as something to serve or please you, you are not really loving him but only yourself. You do not consider the value and dignity that your partner has as a human person. A husband is used as a thing if he is married only as a ticket for financial security; a wife is used as a thing if she is married only to provide sexual satisfaction. These are clear ways of considering the partner as a thing, but there are many more subtle ways of disregarding the rights, feelings, and sensitivities of the other. Animals and material beings are things; human beings are free, responsible beings with their own value and dignity.

This respect for the other as a person means a willingness to leave him in his otherness. Sometimes there is a desire and effort to change the partner into one's own image and likeness. This again is self love, not love of the partner. You married him because he was who he was. Don't try to make drastic changes in his personality. Only try to help him improve his strong points and work on his weak ones. Respect him for what he is, a unique person whom you love.

2. *Develop common interests.*

Love must be built upon common ideals and interests that unite the husband and wife. There is an old axiom: "Love either finds or makes alike." That is so true in happy marriages. Lovers are attracted by what they have in common and this interest must be deepened and extended. Unless this is done the husband and wife will gradually drift away from each other. Try to be interested in and, if possible, share in the partner's hobbies. Play and recreation are wonderful forces to draw and keep people together. Interests cover a wide field depending on the various tastes and opportunities. Religion, politics, civic improvement, education, social work, active sports, and spectator sports are some of the basic areas of interest that can be developed.

3. *Be thoughtful, considerate, forgiving.*

It takes an effort to be thoughtful of the other as each person finds it much easier to think of self. Selfishness is a basic problem in marriage. Insofar as any generalization is true, there is a difference between the selfishness of a man and woman. Being human, both partners will tend to be selfish, and forgetfulness is one of its signs. A man may forget an anniversary; a woman may forget about a business engagement her husband mentioned months before. Much depends on the area of concern. No one has a monopoly on selfishness or forgetfulness. Therefore both husband and wife must go beyond themselves to consider the needs and feelings of the other.

Love is also forgiving. True love can rise above even the hurt inflicted to see the real need of the partner. This is very clearly seen in the woman who learned that her husband was having an affair with another woman. She was able to go beyond her own hurt and ask a priest: "Please, Father, help Johnny." Love does not keep alive the wounds of the past by keeping them in the heart or on the tongue.

4. *Observe the order of love.*

A happy marriage demands that you understand and follow the priorities of love. This is the order of preference in marriage: 1) yourself; 2) your partner; 3) your children; 4) your father, mother, brothers and sisters. If this order is understood it can prevent many problems or settle many difficulties.

It may strike you as strange that you should love yourself ahead of your partner and children. But this is absolutely true. Married love is a love of friendship between a husband and wife as well as a Christian love between a Christian husband and wife. Unless you love and respect yourself you really have nothing to give to your partner. It is not much of a gift to offer yourself when you do not even like yourself. The rule is to love your neighbor as you love yourself. Unless you love yourself as a child of God with definite good qualities you will not know how to love your neighbor.

Your first neighbor is your partner. He comes ahead of the children as the primary relationship is between husband and wife. You will be husband and wife before you are father and mother and you will remain husband and wife when the children are grown and gone. If a man and woman have only the children in common, they are missing the basic joy of marriage and will be lonely and bored when old. It is too late to become husband and wife when the children are no longer present in the home. A husband and wife who are not really getting along will often run away from each other and give all their love to the children. A man can become more a businessman and a wife can become more a mother. If this happens they are miles apart from each other.

Your children are the second in the list of your neighbors. You should love both your partner and your children and not be forced to make a choice to love either your partner or your children. A mature love has room for both. Your love for each other will overflow into love for the children born of your love.

The third line of neighbors is the family in which you were born and raised. Again it should not have to be a choice between your partner and your father or mother. Love for all is compatible as long as the order of preference is maintained. In conflict the principle for decision is found in the first book of the Bible: "A man leaves his father and mother and clings to his wife and the two shall become one flesh" (Gn 2:24).

5. *Love even when you do not like.*

To love means to understand and help even when you do not like what the other is doing. A nagging wife, an alcoholic husband are not likeable but are still lovable. There will be big things that you will not like and which you must help your partner overcome. There will be many small things which you will not like and which your partner will not be able to control because they are so much a part of his temperament. These must be overlooked and not allowed to turn into a serious dislike or even a lessening of love.

To know that one is loved is one of the great blessings of God. It is wonderful to know that you as a person, that your joys and your sorrows really do matter to your partner. Joys are heightened and sorrows lightened by sharing with one who understands and cares.

True and mature love does all things well. What St. Augustine said about man's love of God can be applied to human love: "Love and then do what you will."

chapter 8
talk and listen

In your marriage you are called to become "one in mind, one in heart, and one in affections." This oneness is achieved by personal communication, an openness to each other.

Marriage counselors report that a happy marriage is one in which a husband and wife talk and listen to each other. An unhappy marriage is one in which a husband and wife do not talk and listen. This may seem to be too simple a test for happiness and unhappiness in marriage. But experience shows that talking and listening draw a husband and wife so close to each other that no problem or difficulty can separate them. A marriage counselor is needed when the communication lines are closed or clogged. In such a situation a husband and wife do not talk but either shout in anger or retreat behind the wall of silence. Their relationship becomes a series of bitter, stormy sessions. A marriage counselor serves as a bridge by which each may enter into the other, understand each other, and begin again to love.

Why Don't They Talk?

One of the difficulties in the fast and hurried pace of modern living is that husband and wife are not together often enough for leisurely conversation. There is not enough time to talk. They are together at the worst possible times of the day, in the confusion of the morning and the weariness of the evening. Mother has become a chauffeur who drops off, waits for, or picks up children who are involved in an incredible number of activities. Father spends so much time fighting the traffic to and from work that he arrives home tired and hungry. He just wants to sit and relax and does not feel like making conversation. Besides one's work there are so many activities and affairs that drain off time that the husband and wife just are not able to sit down and talk in a relaxed way.

Sometimes they don't talk because they don't think it is necessary. They blindly follow slogans "Time will take care of it," "The less said the better," "Let sleeping dogs lie," "Talking only leads to argument," "I'll just forget about it and not let it bother me."

Unfortunately time usually makes bad things worse. Time of itself, unless aided by effort, does not work to the advantage of the couple. Things that are not aired or ventilated can create an inner turbulence which explodes in full-blown anger. Hurtful and not easily forgotten words are shouted at each other.

Differences Between Sexes

Some differences in the outlook also can add to the difficulty. Wives often feel that men should sense what is wrong. But normally men are not as perceptive as women and need to have things spelled out very clearly for them. When something is very plain to the woman she takes it for granted that it is just as plain with the man. This is not always true.

Men can also be great dodgers. They don't like to be pushed into conversational corners and they use all kinds of tricks to avoid this. They operate on the premise that if the matter can be dodged for a while the wife will forget about it. They feel that domestic crises, like summer storms, will wear themselves out and do little damage if the husband can just keep out of his wife's way until she cools off.

Nothing to Say

Another reason why couples do not talk is because they have nothing to say. They have grown bored and have not built up common interests. Perhaps they have fed so much on each other and have not grown through reading, new friendships, hobbies, and recreations that they have drained each other and have nothing new to say. They sometimes say that you can always spot a married couple in a restaurant because they are sitting in silence and watching others. A husband and wife possibly can be self-sufficient in the very early days of their marriage but they soon exhaust each other's store of information and interests.

You must develop common interests in sports, recreations, hobbies, and intellectual pursuits. Not that each must actively participate in all activities of the partner but they must keep an active interest in them. If the husband and wife are very interested in bowling and the wife injures her back, there is no need for her to lose her interest in her husband's bowling. But he, too, should become interested in a hobby that she develops to take the place of bowling.

Nonverbal Communication

It is true that a man and woman cannot live together without knowing each other to some extent. But their chief source of information can be limited to what they see and observe in each other. They know each other in the same way as they would know schoolmates or fellow employees. But this knowledge is too impersonal to have much value in marriage. Self-revelation which throws back the curtains that shroud a person's inner thoughts and emotions produces the warm personal knowledge that is so necessary for marriage. Almost every couple learns to read storm signals and to act accordingly. They know when the other is mad or angry and when a blowup is coming and try to avoid it. But things should not be allowed to build up until they erupt in volcanic action.

How to Communicate

1. *Keep talking.* Silence is the greatest possible barrier to communication. It is more effective than an

iron curtain in dividing husband and wife. The way to understand each other is to talk and listen. If a husband and wife can keep up casual and informal conversation, nothing will be allowed to build up out of all proportion. A slight misunderstanding that is not aired can be nursed into a serious grievance. When this finally explodes, both may say things that hurt deeply and are not easily forgotten. Regular sharing keeps the lines of communication open so that small differences may not become large ones, and large ones do not become even larger because kept to oneself.

Such talking should not be merely an occasional event that calls for special attention. If a wife tells her husband as he leaves for work: "I have something I want to talk to you about when you come home tonight," she has quite probably spoiled the day for both of them. Love is the atmosphere in which husband and wife cannot only discuss but disagree. If there is no love, the disagreement becomes an angry defense of one's own position and a stubborn refusal to see the other person's point of view. Each must be careful to listen and answer calmly. Nothing is more frustrating than to have another person walk away when you wish to talk to him.

2. *Keep your temper.* Strange to say, those who love, when angry, can hurt each other the most, and insert the needle in the most sensitive spot. An aroused temper instinctively zeros in on an exposed nerve. One old couple maintained that they had kept their marriage happy because they never allowed themselves to get angry at the same time. If one was angry, the other would make every effort to keep his temper until the other had cooled off.

Emotional words like "stupid" and "foolish" should be avoided at all cost. Such words deeply offend and are not easily forgotten. A husband and wife should have some favorite trick, a word or action, which can serve as a reminder that their tempers are starting to flare. If one can remember this trick at the right moment, the other's anger will not be allowed to increase.

3. *Keep the discussion current.* Don't go back into prehistory to dig up things that were said or done many years ago: "On our first date" — "At the Christmas party of 1967" — "At the wedding reception." Let the past be buried; be ready to forgive and also to forget. If such things are not forgotten, they will readily come out in moments of anger.

4. *Keep it to yourself.* Two are enough for a good discussion or even for a fight. Don't bring in the in-laws, friends, or neighbors. This will only aggravate the situation, lead to no real solution, and often cause future trouble. The wife will more easily forget what her husband has said or done than will her mother to whom she has revealed it. If her husband realizes that she has told all to her mother, he is not going to feel too comfortable when he meets his mother-in-law again. Marital problems are strictly personal and should be revealed only to those who can help. Relatives are not usually the ones who can give proper advice and assistance.

Communication is absolutely necessary if the husband and wife are to receive the happiness God promised them in the sacramental life of marriage. Two must become one, and yet each must be left in his or her otherness. There must be great respect for each other's personality. Each has certain defects that must be accepted.

Communication comes easier to some people than to others, but it is a necessary condition for all happy marriages. Each one must work at it, so that they can become truly "one in mind, one in heart, and one in affection."

chapter 9
the meaning of sex

Sex is an important element in human love and it is

necessary to have an accurate knowledge of the facts as well as a clear realization of its meaning and value. This chapter will explain the meaning and value. The next chapter will present an explanation of the facts of sex.

False Attitudes

Basically there are two false and extreme attitudes toward sex, paganism and puritanism. Paganism holds that the human person is composed only of a human body that will die. There is no soul that will live beyond the grave. Hence when a man's body dies he ceases to be. He may remain in the memory of others, but he himself will no longer exist. This philosophy can lead to the gratification of the human body. If there is no soul, then the body is everything. Hence sex as a part of the human body is to be indulged according to one's desires. Sex is a pleasure to be enjoyed, a thing to be done. The one sin is conception. Hence premarital intercourse and extramarital affairs are taken for granted as long as one does not get "caught." Sex then basically is a thing, an "it" to be enjoyed according to the desires of the individual.

Puritan

On the other hand the puritan viewpoint is equally one-sided. This holds that the body is not an essentially good part of human nature. It is "depraved" and hence something basically evil. Only the soul and "pure things" are good. Hence sex is an evil that is tolerated in marriage either to conceive a child or to please the partner. One who has this attitude talks about sex in terms of debt, duty, and refusal or nonrefusal. A puritan, too, often avoids sex in any way possible, such as by alleging tiredness or by an earlier or later retirement than the partner's.

Both of these extreme attitudes are wrong. One holds that the human body alone is important, the other that the human soul alone is important. They divide what God has united. They miss the whole point of living in an incarnational world in which God, the pure Spirit, became a man with a human body and a human soul. Either philosophy pursued to its logical conclusion destroys the individual because it denies the rights and needs of one element in the human person. It is only at our own risk that we try to divide what God has brought together.

God's View

God's view is that human love must be human. This means that both the soul and the body must have their rightful place in the expression of human love. Sex is the total gift of oneself, soul and body, to one's partner.

Since body and soul are the essential elements of human nature both must be present in married love. Neither the gift of souls alone nor of bodies alone would be human because it is only partial. A person is neither body nor soul alone but both together united in a unique human being. God wanted both elements present and hence made man more passionate so that he could more easily take the initiative in the union of bodies; he made the woman more affectionate so that she could more easily take the lead in the union of souls. Man can teach woman the physical pleasure found in love; woman can make known the spiritual joy of married love. Each must learn from the other because each has a body and soul that must enter willingly and generously into married love. Each also must take the initiative in both unions. A man wants to be wanted and a wife should initiate love-making at times. A woman wants to feel that her husband loves all of her and hence he must also take the lead in the union of souls. Anything completely one-sided in marriage is wrong. This principle applies in all areas: care of the house, discipline of children, and the sexual expression of married love.

Development of Love

All love leads to union, a desire to be united with the loved one as intimately as possible. There are various steps in the development of love that lead to its full expression in the love act of intercourse.

1. *Internally:* first of all a lover desires to be with the loved one in thought and desire. When you love you are constantly thinking of the one you love. If a girl and a boy are separated by his military service for his country, their thoughts are constantly with each other. In this way they seek to bridge the gap of distance. They can hardly wait for a letter, a phone call, a furlough, discharge.

2. *Externally:* the desire for union must lead to a real union with the loved one. A strong desire will show itself in action. A lover wishes to give presents and especially himself to the one he loves. There are three basic gifts which reveal clearly the development of love.

The first gift is something distinct from yourself, a present which has value because it comes from one who loves. Candy, flowers, ties, etc., are thoughtful expressions of love which have a far greater value than their objective worth. They are signs of thoughtful love. Incidentally, these small presents should be continued after marriage which thrives on such small meaningful gifts.

Next the lover gives himself either partially or fully. Affection is a partial gift of oneself, as a kiss is not merely a union of bodies, of lips, but a union of souls. The kiss has meaning between the lover and the loved one.

This affectionate or partial gift leads to the passionate or full gift in the complete love act of intercourse.

There is a progression in the manifestation of love. First a gift distinct from self, then the partial gift of self and finally the full gift of self.

Principles of Married Love

1. *The complete gift of self in the love act of intercourse is good and holy.*

Sex is not shameful but good and holy because created by God for a wonderful purpose and elevated by Christ to the dignity of a sacrament. Through sex a husband and wife share in the creative power of God.

The conception of a baby is the result of three loves: God's, the husband's, and the wife's. God surely would not cooperate with an action that was not good. The sex act is also an expression of the love of the husband and wife for each other, and all true love comes from God and leads to him.

The love act of intercourse is also holy because it is the expression, the fulfillment of the sacrament of Matrimony. We do not know exactly when Christ raised marriage to the level of a sacrament. It might have been when he attended the marriage feast at Cana, or when he forbade man to put asunder what God has joined together. But it is true that when you and your husband give yourselves to each other you draw closer not only to each other but to Christ. Intercourse is a sacred action of the sacrament of Matrimony just as the Consecration of the bread and wine is a sacred act of the sacrament of Holy Orders. Another way of expressing the holiness of married love is to say that its expression is a good action which increases sanctifying grace in the soul.

A quick and spontaneous answer to an unusual question will usually reveal clearly how you feel about sex in marriage. The question: Suppose you were making love and, in some impossible manner, learned that you had five minutes left to live, what would you do? Would you continue love-making, or would you stop and pray? (The answer must be given at once without any reflection to try to discover what the right answer is.) A spontaneous reply will ordinarily show your true, if unconscious, feelings about sex. The correct answer, of course, is to continue love-making which is the living of the sacrament of Matrimony, and which draws you closer not only to each other but also to Christ. The closer you are to Christ in this world the closer you will be to him in heaven.

The question is adopted from the one asked of a saint who was taking recreation: "What would you do if you knew you had five minutes to live?" His answer: "I would continue relaxing because I am taking necessary recreation." The point of the example is that if the saint would continue doing something which was an indifferent action in itself, how much more should a married couple continue their love-making which is an action good in itself.

To understand this point better you must realize that there are three classes of human actions: good, bad, indifferent. A list of good actions would include: Holy Communion, marital intercourse, prayer, charity. Among the bad actions would be stealing, adultery, hatred, and lying. The indifferent actions would be things like tennis, golf, football, etc. The indifferent actions can become either good or bad depending on the intention and circumstances. The point is that if the saint would continue an indifferent action which needs a good intention to make it a good human act, how much more should the married couple continue love-making which is good in itself and does not need the influence of a good intention to make it good.

2. *Intimate love-making, kissing, embracing, touching, as preparation for the complete love act is good and holy and necessary.*

This intimate love-making is a very normal and natural part of love. Just as there is nothing shameful about the complete gift of self in married love there is nothing shameful in the preparatory actions. These actions are normal expressions of human love. They, too, increase sanctifying grace in the husband and wife.

These acts of love are a necessary preparation because the full gift is prepared for by the partial gift of self. These actions lead to the full gift of self in a twofold way. Psychologically, when you give you want to give more and more. Physiologically, sex is touch, and repeated touches lead to the intimate contact of intercourse. A woman who is more affectionate needs this love-making to lead her to the passionate which is the full gift of self. Husbands, sometimes, do not realize their wife's great need for affection to prepare them for the passionate.

The connection between the affectionate and the

passionate will help engaged couples to understand why they may have some trouble in restraining their love. Sex never really becomes a problem until you love and want to show your love. Gradually this love creeps over the boundary into the preserve of married love. A boy and girl can really try to keep these expressions of married love for their proper place but human weakness is often a factor. The good God can understand and forgive human weakness.

There is some danger that a couple may have a sense of guilt over sex itself and not over its stolen expression. In this connection it is important to remember the three S's: Sex, Sacred, Stolen. Only in the context of the sacred can sex be properly evaluated. Sex before marriage is wrong not because it is dirty but because it is stolen. If a person feels that sex is dirty in itself, all that marriage can do is to whitewash it. Marriage only makes sex legal for such a person. Psychologically, it is very difficult if not impossible to feel right about doing dirty actions even if they are legal.

3. *Love-making, intimate kissing, touching, embracing, even when not in preparation for the complete love act, is good and holy provided neither climaxes.*

Love-making is not reserved only as preparation for the complete marital love act. It should be shown at other times. The only condition is that full sexual satisfaction belongs only in full sexual love. Occasionally a climax may be reached accidentally and unintentionally outside of intercourse, but you would not be morally responsible for this.

God made sex as the gift of the soul and body in the holiness of married love. Its value and meaning can come only from the God who made it and elevated it to its sacramental status.

chapter 10
anatomy

Knowledge of the sexual organs and their functions is

normal and necessary for the husband and wife. It is important also to know and use the proper terms, as gutter language degrades sex. One of the early saints of the Church, St. Clement of Alexandria, said: "We should not be ashamed to name that which God was not ashamed to create." No part of the body is bad; each part is good and has a proper name. Incidentally, if you know the correct terms you will be better able to instruct your children. The proper name also helps build a proper attitude toward sex.

Size

There is no definite size for these organs. Sometimes people feel that their organs are too small or too large. As in all human things, there are relative sizes. The size has nothing to do with the function. The penis, no matter what size, is made to enter the vagina and deposit the seed there. The vagina, no matter what its size, is made to receive the penis and the seed and also to enlarge to allow the baby to be born. There is no reason to worry about size. If, for instance, the penis is too large for the vagina, by careful consideration and tact the vagina is capable of being enlarged to receive it. Also, if the breasts are small, there is no need to wonder whether one has milk enough to nurse. The size of the breast has nothing to do with its milk-producing qualities.

The Male Shape

The upper half of a man's body is generally broad and muscular and his hips are usually smaller. This enables him to do heavier work and to protect his wife and children. His muscles are of a rougher texture and tend to bulge more and give him his characteristic male shape. The male distribution of hair is on his face, chest, under the arms, and in the pubic area where it extends upward and pointedly to the navel. This hair is also spread sparsely over the rest of his body.

The Penis

The penis and the scrotum are the two external male

sex organs. The penis hangs from the pelvis. The tip or end of the penis contains the gland that is the source of sex pleasure in the male. This is covered with a foreskin. Often the male is circumcised — the foreskin is cut away — so that the seed cannot accumulate there. The penis assumes two states; it is either soft or erect. In the erected state it stands out from the body and the tip is filled with blood so that it is very sensitive to touch. It is only in the erect state that it is able to enter the vagina.

The Urethra

This is a tubelike passageway which travels from the bladder through the entire length of the penis. It serves both for the passage of urine and seminal fluid. It is impossible, normally, to pass both urine and seminal fluid at the same time.

The Scrotum

The scrotum is the external sac or pouch which contains the testicles. The pouch is divided into a left and right compartment with one testicle in each section. The outer part is composed of skin and specialized muscle. Its appearance varies according to circumstances. Under the influence of warmth, old age, or sickness, it becomes relaxed and longer; under the influence of impending danger or injury by a blow or cold temperatures it becomes tight and it draws the testicles toward the pelvis for protection and warmth to save these delicate organs. The scrotum is sparsely covered with hair not necessarily for warmth but as feelers comparable to a cat's whiskers to warn of impending dangers.

Testicles

The scrotum forms a sac for the two testicles. The testicles are two glands with a twofold function, the external secretion of the seed and the internal secretion of the hormone.

The seeds or sperm cells are deposited in the female vagina and the number of sperms in a single ejaculation varies between 300 to 500 million. The sperm cell contains a body and a tail. Under a microscope they look like polywogs swimming about and actually do swim in the seminal fluid. They live about forty-eight hours after ejaculation or discharge into the vagina. This cell, like all cells, is composed mainly of proteins, the food substances and the cell builders. The sperm of the man and the egg of the woman carry the traits of heredity.

The Hormones

The internal secretions of the testicles or hormones are absorbed into the blood stream and influence the pitch of the man's voice, the distribution of his hair, his general masculine shape — broad shoulders and narrow hips — muscular texture and strength and the male attitude of aggression toward the female.

The Female Sex Organs

The whole sexual apparatus of the woman is to help her conceive, carry, and deliver a child as well as to make her responsive to the man in their mutual love so that it becomes an enjoyable experience for both of them.

The Female Shape

It is both functional and attractive to man. It is functional because of the broad hips for the carrying and delivering of infants. It is attractive because it is curvaceous, soft, and tender.

The Distribution of Hair

A woman has hair on the head, under the arms, and around the sex organs. This pubic hair is lesser than in the male and it ends abruptly in the uppermost part, while the male distribution extends upward toward the navel. The rest of the female body has very light fuzzy covering.

The Breasts

The primary purpose of the breast is to provide milk

for the child. It is also a secondary sexual gland. The size and dimensions vary from person to person as well as according to age. They begin to develop about the age of twelve. They enlarge during pregnancy and become even larger after childbirth especially when secreting milk. They decrease in size after the menopause. They consist of skin, fat, milk glands, and blood vessels. The nipple is capable of sexual excitation and becomes erect as does the penis or the clitoris. The color of the nipple varies from pink in a woman who has never had a child or been pregnant to very dark brown in a woman who either is or has been pregnant.

The Labia

The labia, or genital lips, are part of the external female sex organs and are simply folds of mucous membranes like the lining of the mouth. These major and minor lips cover the other sexual organs. Upon sexual excitation, they become filled with blood, enlarge, and relax. This together with the secretions of the glands makes for easier and painless insertion of the penis for intercourse. A husband should realize this and be considerate enough to stimulate his wife so that this flow makes intercourse easier and more desirable.

The Clitoris

The clitoris is a small organ made of the same spongy-like tissue as the penis. But it is much smaller than the penis and also has no connection with the bladder. It is partially hidden next to the urinary opening. It appears pinkish in color and is about the size of a small pea. The clitoris is a very sensitive organ and erects or hardens under sexual excitation and usually is the main center of sexual stimulation for the woman.

The Vagina

The vagina is the tubelike organ that leads to the womb. It is the birth canal, the recipient of the penis during intercourse, and the passageway for the menstrual flow. It is capable of enormous dilation dur-

The hymen or maidenhead is a thin fold of mucous membrane across the opening of the vagina. This only partially covers the vagina and does not impede the menstrual flow. It is stretched or ruptured by intercourse or by any violent physical forms of exercise. In most girls this is broken before marriage because of the great activity of the modern girl. Hence a broken hymen is no indication or proof that a girl has had intercourse.

The Uterus or Womb

The womb is a hollow thick-walled muscular organ situated in the pelvis between the urinary bladder and the rectum. It is best visualized as an inverted pear. The upper and larger part has tubes leading to the ovaries; the lower part is connected with the vagina. The uterus houses the fertilized egg for nine months prior to birth and continues to grow as the baby grows. At the ninth month the uterus fills almost the entire abdominal cavity and has pushed the other organs aside. At term, about 280 days, the uterus begins to contract (labor pains) aided by the abdominal muscles in a rhythmical fashion until the baby is slowly pushed through the birth canal (the vagina) to the outside world. After the uterus is empty of the baby and the afterbirth (the placenta) it contracts down to near normal size.

The cervix or the lower part of the uterus is cone shaped. It contains an opening to the vagina. Its size varies according to whether the woman has had children or not. Usually the vagina is smaller in a person who has not had a child, and this sometimes accounts for painful menstruation.

The Tubes

The Fallopian tubes are on both sides of the uterus. These organs are about three inches in length and the open end of the tube is a little bit smaller than the size of a lead in a pencil. The end of each tube contains loose ends or hairlike tentacles; the inner side contains cilia or hairlike projections. When the egg is freed by the ovary into the pelvis the hairlike ends are constantly in motion; they pick up the egg and place it in the tube where the inside hairs project it toward the uterus. If the egg is not fertilized, it is absorbed by the tissues of the uterus as are the unused male sperm cells.

The Ovaries

These are the female counterpart of the male testicles. They are about the size of an olive and are situated in the pelvis on either side of the uterus or womb. The ovaries are readily movable and make room for the enlarging womb in pregnancy.

The Egg

The egg, which is formed every month, is the external product of the ovaries. Each ovary forms an egg every other month. Thus it is possible for a woman with only one ovary to conceive a child. The egg lives about twenty-four hours after it has been released by the ovary. If male seeds are present when the egg descends into the tube it can be penetrated by one of the seeds and conception takes place. After conception the fertilized egg moves slowly toward the womb and arrives at about the fourth day. It then implants itself in the wall of the womb and continues to grow and develop for nine months.

Hormones

The female hormones are secreted by the ovaries into the bloodstream. They regulate the menstrual cycle, the pitch of the voice, the contours of the body, the development of the breasts, the distribution of hair, the texture of the skin, the strength of the muscles, the broadness of the hips.

Menstruation

Adult women menstruate on an average at monthly intervals unless impeded by some disturbance. This time is called their period. A woman during pregnancy does not menstruate. The mechanics of menstruation are controlled by the hormones. The hormones stimulate the ovaries to produce the egg about fifteen days before the period. Some women are aware of the fact that they are ovulating. At this time the woman is more interested in love-making. She becomes more vivacious and alluring. Her husband is sometimes unconsciously or consciously aware of the fact of ovulation and is especially attracted to his wife. This is nature's way of telling both of them that this is the best possible time for conception.

The womb that is not impregnated will in a few weeks begin the menstrual flow. Each month the uterus prepares for pregnancy. When this ambition is frustrated, the lining of the uterus and the accumulated blood stored for this purpose break down and are discharged by gravity and muscular contractions. This is nature's method to prepare for a possible pregnancy during the next cycle. After the menstruation another lining grows with the same accumulation of blood awaiting for new life to be implanted therein. Sometimes painful menstrual flows can be caused by too small an opening in the cervix which serves as a dam and prevents the uterus from emptying itself. This results in painful cramps.

God has made the sexual organs and functions so that a man and woman may show their love for each other and cooperate in the conception of a child. Knowledge of sex takes away fear caused by ignorance. In case of doubts ask your doctor for further explanation. A couple who are expecting a baby should know very much about the wonderful event that is taking place.

chapter 11
the art of love-making

Once you have the proper attitude toward sex and know the nature and functions of the sex organs you should understand some of the basic principles of love-making. Love is a giving and a receiving which make the husband and wife one.

Sex must be an expression of love or it is a horrible experience, especially for the wife. Sex has to be: "I need and want you and I give myself to you." Sex is always personal and never an it. Sex is human love, a gift of the total personality, soul and body, to the partner.

Test of Marriage

Marriage is much more than physical sex, but sex is so important that it is a good test of a marriage. If a couple are adjusted sexually it is a very good sign that they are adjusted in other ways. Sexual adjustment comes from personal adjustment and leads to greater personal adjustment. If a husband and wife get along in the bedroom, it is because they are getting along in other rooms.

A successful marriage counselor considers sex as a barometer of marriage. When people complain that their marriage is in trouble he quickly asks them about their sexual adjustment. If this is good, he knows that any problems must be minor ones because major problems would quickly show up in the sex area. If there is a lack of sexual adjustment, he knows there must be real trouble somewhere. He checks to see if the problem is in the sex area because of a lack of proper attitude. For example, frigidity in the man or woman is in almost all cases caused by a fear of sex in itself or a fear of pregnancy. But usually the problem is in another area. The counselor's task is to help the people uncover the real cause and take the proper steps to settle the difficulty and work out a happy marriage.

An Art

Love-making is not something to be learned from books. It is rather an art to be discovered in mutual love. It is true that some knowledge of technique can be of assistance but only in the service of love. Sex cannot be understood primarily as a duty to be endured or a pleasure to be enjoyed, but as an expression of human love. This is not to deny that duty and pleasure are involved, but love must be present to make sex what it should be. In their love a couple try to understand more of the mystery of the other, to discover ways to please, means to intensify their love. Sex cannot really be enjoyed if one is angry with the other, though one can rise above anger in giving self to the other. Sex is communication, and by word and response each must make known to the other what is enjoyable and helps their love for each other.

This discussion can be divided into three parts: 1) *the fore play,* 2) *the love act itself,* 3) *the after play.*

The Fore Play

A man is usually easily aroused sexually. The thought of love, the sight of his wife's body, a touch can arouse a man and make him ready for intercourse. A woman, on the contrary, is slowly aroused. She must love her husband and love him at the moment; she must be held, kissed, and fondled so that she becomes ready in body and soul for intercourse. If this were to be graphed, a male chart would show a quick arousing and equally rapid descent. The female chart would reveal a slow ascent and after several minutes a minor descent with another ascent to the climax and a slow descent while her organs are returning to their normal state.

Morally, any touch, kiss, embrace that prepares the husband and wife for the mutual gift of themselves in intercourse is good and holy. Psychologically, the particular actions depend so much on the attitude of the husband and wife. Sometimes in the early days of marriage a husband and a wife are not quite ready for more intimate touching and kissing. The husband and wife must show delicate sensitiveness for the feelings of each other and not force a morally good action on the other until both are prepared for it. But it is very important that this feeling does not arise from an attitude that sex is not too nice or from ignorance about what is morally permissible. So often ignorance and an improper attitude go together and create problems in marriage. Both the ignorance and the attitude can be overcome by a realization on an intellectual and emotional level that these touches, kisses, etc., are very normal signs of love, are morally permissible, and are the living of the sacrament of Matrimony. Each can help the other by trying to understand the attitude and gently trying to aid the other in forming the correct attitude. Force in this situation only intensifies the feeling that these actions are really not love but only selfish efforts to receive more pleasure from sex without real love and concern for the other.

Erotic Areas

It does help a young couple to know the sensitive areas in self and the other. The primary erotic centers in the man are the penis and the testicles; the primary centers in the woman are the nipples, the external sex organs, and particularly the clitoris. In both the man and the woman the lips, the neck, ears, and thighs are the secondary sex areas. These areas should be touched, fondled, kissed. It is wise to begin with the secondary centers and work toward the primary. But a word of caution is useful here. Love-making is a very personal matter that should not follow any particular pattern. It depends so much on the feelings of the moment. Love should be spontaneous. This means it will vary from time to time.

Privacy

Love-making as a personal act demands privacy. This can be difficult if the young couple are living with others and the fear of being discovered in love can prevent a total gift of self. Also privacy must be safeguarded when your own children come.

Sometimes a false modesty disturbs the freedom of love. A desire to make love only in darkness can arise from a feeling that sex is not too nice. Or a reluctance to fully unclothe during love-making can result from a general uneasiness about sex. To see each other as God made you is perfectly natural.

The husband should always remember his wife's great need of affection to get her ready for intercourse. In the beginning it may be difficult for him to control himself so that he can wait for her. Control can be achieved by concentrating more upon his wife than upon himself.

Intercourse

When the husband and wife feel that they are both ready for intercourse the husband should insert his penis into the vagina of his wife. The wife knows that she is prepared if her clitoris has been stimulated and there is a lubricating fluid present in the vagina. Her readiness should be communicated by word or action to her husband.

The climax or full sexual satisfaction in the male consists of muscular contractions of the penis which result in the discharge of the seed into the vagina. After this happens the penis loses its hardness and the blood returns to the bloodstream. The wife's climax is a series of rhythmic contractions of the clitoris which lead to a peak release of tension. After this her organs relax, but not as quickly as the husband's organ. There may also be a climax in the vagina through the muscular contractions of the walls of the vagina in harmony with the contractions of the man's penis.

It will take time for a satisfactory sexual adjustment to be realized. The man in the early days of the marriage may climax too soon so that he loses the seed outside the vagina. There is no need to worry, as this is an accident and God does not hold one responsible for accidents. It may take some time after marriage before a wife is able to reach a climax, and possibly still longer before she climaxes at the same time as her husband.

A climax is an important part of marriage, but not nearly as important as some people make it. Sometimes ideas get distorted so that the true purpose of intercourse is forgotten. Love and not climax is the purpose of intercourse. When people become preoccupied with climax — the husband to make sure his wife enjoys their love, the wife to be certain that she climaxes to reach fulfillment as well as please her husband — sex is out of focus. Climax is a normal result of love, hence the emphasis should be on showing love and let the climax come naturally.

The man's climax should be reached while united with his wife. Her climax may be attained at any time during the total love act — before her husband, at the same time, or afterward. Husbands should be considerate in their love-making to help the wife reach fulfillment; wives should not try to fool their husbands by pretending they reach a climax when they don't.

After Play

The husband and wife should continue to love each other after they have reached their orgasms. Surely if the wife has not reached her orgasm the husband should make love to her until she does. But again this should not be a great project that would take a long, long period of time — which is only frustrating to both the husband and wife. This should be guided by the desires of the wife. But the husband should not turn over and go to sleep immediately. He should continue to hold his wife in his arms and make love to her. This is a wonderful time to communicate and tell how one really feels about the other.

Sex is and can be a great part of marriage when viewed as a sign of the love the husband and wife have for each other. All the rules in the world and all the knowledge of various techniques and positions and so forth will not be of any avail unless the act of intercourse is a love act between two people who really love and give themselves to each other. Any difficulties or misunderstandings should be talked about just as any other problems in the marriage should be openly discussed. Remember that the husband and wife are two in one flesh, and at that precise moment they are a

sign and symbol also of the intimate union of Christ with
his Church.

chapter 12
responsible parenthood

You realize the importance of children in marriage
but there are so many questions that may come to your
mind. Which comes first, the love of the husband and
wife for each other or the conception and care of
children? When should children be born? How many?
Should families be planned? How many children are
sufficient? Who is to determine the number of children?
Is family planning wrong? What is the Church's attitude
on birth control? How about the pill? How can we
afford Catholic education for our children?

These and many other questions must be asked and
answered by a young couple before marriage. Their
consciences must be formed with the guidance of the
teaching authority of the Church.

The material in this chapter is divided into three
sections. 1) *the personal and the parental goals in
marriage,* 2) *responsible parenthood,* 3) *birth control.*

Personal and Parental Goals

In marriage the husband and wife find love and
fulfillment in each other and in their children. Theologians debate about the relationship between personal
love and procreation of children. There is no need to
enter into this controversy except to say that both
elements are found in marriage.

Vatican II studiously avoids using the old terms of
primary and secondary purposes of marriage, but
clearly shows the close connection between children
and love. "By their very nature, the institution of
Matrimony itself and conjugal love are ordained for the
procreation and education of children, and find in them

their ultimate crown" *(Church in the Modern World,* n. 48).

"Marriage and conjugal love are by their very nature ordained toward the begetting and educating of children. Children are really the supreme gift of marriage. Hence while not making the other purposes of Matrimony of less account, the true practice of conjugal love and the whole meaning of the family life which results from that, have this aim: that the couple be ready with stout hearts to cooperate with the love of the Creator and the Savior who through them will enlarge and enrich his own family day-by-day" *(Church in the Modern World,* n. 50).

Pope Paul VI in his well-known encyclical, *Human Life,* explains that the teaching of the Church is based on:

". . . the inseparable connection, willed by God and unable to be broken by man on his own initiative, between the two meanings of the conjugal act: the unitive meaning and the procreative meaning. Indeed, by its intimate structure, the conjugal act, while most closely uniting husband and wife, capacitates them for the generation of new lives, according to laws inscribed in the very being of man and woman. By safeguarding both these essential aspects, the unitive and the procreative, the conjugal act preserves in its fullness the sense of true mutual love and its ordination toward man's most high calling to parenthood" (n. 12).

Thus marriage is love in the service of life. Husband and wife find fulfillment in their love for each other and in children born of that love. True love desires to share and to grow. A husband and wife wish to give themselves to each other and to see that love shared with another human being, the fruit of their love.

Responsible Parenthood

Responsible parenthood is a popular phrase with different meanings. It is used by the promoters of artificial birth control as well as by advocates of natural birth control. Basically, responsible parenthood means that parents must act according to the principles of reason and faith in deciding whether to bring a child into the world.

Paul VI

Pope Paul VI in his encyclical, *Human Life,* states the various responsibilities that must be considered. "The responsible exercise of parenthood implies, therefore, that husband and wife recognize fully their own duties toward God, toward themselves, toward the family, and toward society, in a correct hierarchy of values" (n. 10).

Toward God

The Council Fathers of Vatican II explained this duty of charity toward God.

"Parents should regard as their proper mission the task of transmitting human life and educating those to whom it has been transmitted. They should realize that they are thereby cooperators with the love of God, the Creator, and are, so to speak, the interpreters of that love.

"Thus trusting in divine Providence and refining the spirit of sacrifice, married Christians glorify the Creator and strive toward fulfillment in Christ, when, with a generous human and Christian sense of responsibility, they acquit themselves of the duty to procreate" (*Church in the Modern World,* n. 50).

Thus there is a duty of charity in responsible parenthood to give honor and glory to the Creator by bringing children into the world and making them heirs of heaven by joining them with Christ.

Toward Themselves

In an address of February 12, 1966, Pope Paul VI expresses this duty toward themselves as: "Mutual charity by means of which each seeks the good of the other and tries to anticipate the other's good desires rather than impose his own will."

In the matter of children, as in all other matters, the

decision should be a mutual one. A husband should not insist on another child when the wife would not be able to provide proper care. Nor should the wife demand another child when the husband would not be able to support a larger family. A delicate sensitiveness to the needs of the other should be found in this regard as in all aspects of marriage. If one or the other is opposed to another child, love will not force but gently try to help the other see matters in a different light.

Toward the Family

Vatican II states this responsibility:

"They will thoughtfully take into account both their own welfare and that of their children, those already born and those which may be foreseen. For this accounting they will reckon with both the material and the spiritual conditions of the times as well as of their state in life. Finally, they will consult the interests of the family group, of temporal society, and of the Church itself" (*Church in the Modern World*, n. 50).

Responsible parenthood demands that the parents consider whether they are able to give the love and care needed for the support and education of their children. The physical and emotional health of the father and mother should be taken into account. Family income, the size of the house, and other material factors are an essential part of the picture. Perhaps the presence of a retarded child demands so much care that there is not enough time to give to the other children. Parents could fail against the love owed to an only child by selfishly refusing to give him a brother or sister. This decision is a highly personal one which depends on the nature and capabilities of the husband and wife. What would be a very difficult burden for one would be a joy for another person. You must decide this yourself and not attempt to judge others.

Toward Society

Parents have a responsibility to society because the family is its basic unit. When God established marriage he laid upon man and woman the obligation "to be fruitful and multiply and fill the earth." Society, in its turn, has the responsibility of helping provide sufficient food, suitable housing, necessary education, and everything else required so that the family can lead a true human life.

Who Makes the Decision?

"Parents will fulfill their task with human and Christian responsibility. With docile reverence toward God, they will come to the right decision by common counsel and effort. The parents themselves should ultimately make this judgment, in the sight of God" (*Church in the Modern World,* n. 50).

The number and planning or spacing of children does depend upon the judgment of the husband and wife. They and they alone fully know the circumstances of their life and must judge whether the response should be yes or no.

"But in their manner of acting spouses should be aware that they cannot proceed arbitrarily. They must always be governed according to a conscience dutifully conformed to the divine law itself, and should be submissive toward the teaching authority of the Church, which authentically interprets that law in the light of the gospel" (*Church in the Modern World,* n. 50).

This section on responsible parenthood can be summarized by a quotation from Pope Paul's encyclical *Human Life.*

"In relation to physical, economic, psychological, and social conditions, responsible parenthood is exercised, either by the deliberate and generous decision to raise a numerous family, or by the decision, made for grave motives and with due respect for the moral law, to avoid for the time being, or even for an indeterminate period, a new birth" (n. 10).

Birth Control

Birth control, as is evident, means the control or

regulation of births by the decision of the parents. There are two basic kinds: artificial and natural. Anything done before, during, or after the marital act which prevents the conception of a child is artificial birth control. To explain further. "Anything done before" refers to the use of the "pill" which stops ovulation, or any chemical or mechanical means by the husband or the wife that prevents the male seed from reaching the womb. "During the marital act" refers to the noncompletion of intercourse by the withdrawal of the penis to prevent placing the seed in the vagina. "After the marital act" refers to the use of a douche immediately after intercourse with the purpose of not allowing the seed to reach the womb.

Abortion is the deliberate expulsion of a nonviable fetus from the womb. Doctors refer to a miscarriage as a spontaneous abortion. If a wife loses a baby by miscarriage she should baptize the fetus. If the fetus is sufficiently developed so that it can be recognized, water is poured on the forehead while these words are said: "If you are capable, I baptize you in the name of the Father, the Son, and the Holy Spirit." If the fetus is not sufficiently developed to be recognized and is still enclosed in the membrane, the whole membrane should be placed in water; then the membrane should be opened, and while the miscarriage is moved through the water these words are said: "If you are capable, I baptize you in the name of the Father, the Son, and the Holy Spirit."

Teaching of the Church

The teaching of the Church on both artificial and natural birth control will be given by direct quotation from official documents.

Vatican II

The Second Vatican Council did not directly treat the subject of birth control but it did make some important points: ". . . the moral aspect of any procedure does not depend solely on sincere intention or on an evaluation of motives. It must be determined by objective standards. These, based on the nature of the human person and his acts, preserve the full sense of mutual self-giving and human procreation in the context of true love . . . Relying on these principles, sons of the Church may not undertake methods of regulating procreation which are found blameworthy by the teaching authority of the Church in its unfolding of the divine law" (*Church in the Modern World,* n. 51).

Pope Pius XI

A well-known quotation from the encyclical, *Chaste Wedlock,* presents the doctrine in these words: "Any use whatsoever of Matrimony exercised in such a way that the act is deliberately frustrated in its natural power to generate life is an offense against the law of God and of nature, and those who indulge in such are branded with the guilt of a grave sin" (n. 54).

Pope Paul VI

Human Life, the long awaited encyclical of Pope Paul VI, appeared on July 29, 1968, and reaffirmed the doctrine taught by Pope Pius XI and other popes.

"In the task of transmitting life, therefore, they are not free to proceed completely at will as if they could determine in a wholly autonomous way the morally right path to follow, but they must conform their activity to the creative intention of God, expressed in the very nature of marriage and its acts, and manifested by the constant teaching of the Church (n. 10).

"The Church, calling men back to the observance of the norms of the natural law as interpreted by their constant doctrine, teaches that each and every marriage act must remain open to the transmission of life (n. 11).

"To use this divine gift destroying, even if only partially, its meaning and its purpose is to contradict the nature both of man and of woman and of their most intimate relationship, and therefore it is to contradict also the plan of God and his will (n. 13).

"We must once again declare that the direct

interruption of the generative process already begun, and, above all, directly willed and procured abortion, even if for therapeutic reasons, are to be absolutely excluded as licit means of regulating birth.

"Equally to be excluded, as the teaching authority of the Church has frequently declared, is direct sterilization, whether perpetual or temporary, whether of the man or of the woman. Similarly excluded is every action which, either in anticipation of the conjugal act, or in its accomplishment, or in the development of its natural consequences, proposes, whether as an end or as a means, to render procreation impossible" (n. 14).

There is no doubt that the Church through Pope Pius XI and Pope Paul VI has condemned artificial birth control. While their statements are not infallible they are expressions of the teaching authority of the Church and must be accepted by the members of the Church. In making this difficult decision Pope Paul agonized through many years of prayer, study, and consultation.

In his encyclical he addresses himself directly to Christian husbands and wives.

"We do not at all intend to hide the sometimes serious difficulties inherent in the life of Christian married persons; for them as for everyone else, 'the gate is narrow and the way is hard that leads to life.' But the hope of that life must illumine their way, as with courage they strive to live with wisdom, justice and piety in this present time, knowing that the figure of this world passes away.

"Let married couples, then, face up to the efforts needed, supported by the faith and hope which 'do not disappoint . . . because God's love has been poured into our hearts through the Holy Spirit who has been given to us.' Let them implore divine assistance by persevering prayer; above all let them draw from the source of grace and charity in the Eucharist. And if sin should still keep its hold over them, let them not be discouraged, but rather have recourse with humble perseverance to the mercy of God which is poured forth in the sacrament of Penance" (n. 25).

Rhythm

The rhythm method of natural birth control is a means of regulating births by limiting intercourse to the sterile time of the wife's cycle. A woman is fertile only at the time of ovulation. The problem, then, is to determine the exact time of ovulation. Scientists have proposed various ways to pinpoint ovulation and are doing the research necessary to discover a simple method which would be easily understood and followed.

Pope Paul VI has stated the position of the Church on the use of the rhythm.

"If, then, there are serious motives to space out births, which derive from the physical or psychological conditions of husband and wife, or from external conditions, the Church teaches that it is then licit to take into account the natural rhythms immanent in the generative functions, for the use of marriage in the infecund periods only, and in this way to regulate births without offending the moral principles which have been recalled earlier" *(Human Life,* n. 16).

Information about rhythm should be obtained from your doctor or a Family Life Clinic. It may be difficult to understand a book or pamphlet. Information from a friend may not always be reliable. Go to the proper sources and follow the advice given if you wish to use the rhythm method.

Generosity is always a great quality and the Council has a special passage in praise of it. "Among the couples who fulfill their God-given task in this way, those merit special mention who with wise and common deliberation and with a gallant heart undertake to bring up suitably even a relatively large family" *(Church in the Modern World,* n. 50).

Children contribute much to marriage and responsible parenthood is an essential element in marriage. It is not merely a negative but a positive response to the demands of charity, the duty of love. It may call for sacrifices — great sacrifices at times — but the grace of the sacrament of marriage is always present to help those who respond in love.

Ovulation Method

A comparatively new method of family planning, which in no way contravenes Catholic teaching on marriage, has been introduced in the Archdiocese of Los Angeles by Drs. John and Lynn Billings, a husband-wife team of Australian physicians.

The ovulation method of family planning does not require a knowledge of complex scientific information. It does not require regularity of ovulation nor regularity of a menstrual cycle. There are no drugs nor devices of any kind. The ovulation method is considered natural and in accord with the teachings of the Church. Ideally, it is best taught by women to other women in preference to an explanation by male doctors. To understand this method, some knowledge of the ovarian cycle is necessary. Its accuracy depends upon the identification of a cervical mucus secretion. Unlike the rhythm method, which depends on the regularity of the cycle, in the ovulation method each cycle can be treated as independent of the others. Every time a woman ovulates she will have a recognizable mucus pattern. In order to perceive these changes in the cervical mucus, a woman must learn her own pattern by keeping a daily record for one or two cycles.

Indeed, Dr. Billings contends this method of establishing the limits of the fertile period is both more simple and more sure than other ways of determining these boundaries. Complete information about the ovulation method is contained in *The Ovulation Method*, by Dr. John J. Billings, obtainable from Liturgical Press, St. John's Abbey, Collegeville, MN 56321.

chapter 13
your child

When you marry you look forward to the day when your love will be blessed with a baby. You have seen the your love will be blessed with a baby. You have seen the joy of young couples as they play with their baby and hope, some day, to know the same joy.

Much could be said about a baby. But here only two points will be presented: the miracle that is a baby and the care and discipline of a child.

Human Love

"A baby is born of human love." A husband and wife wish to be united to each other in love and to make visible this love in a baby. To unite and express love is the nature of all love. This is true in the intimate life of the Holy Trinity. The Father and the Son love each other and breathe forth their love in the Holy Spirit who is the expression of the mutual love of the Father and Son for each other. This pattern for all love has been set by God himself because "God is love and all love comes from him." The love of the couple in cooperation with the creative omnipotence of God brings about the loving conception of the child.

This love manifests itself in many ways during the nine months of pregnancy. Love leads the young mother-to-be to make many sacrifices during these days. The sacrifices are necessary to safeguard the physical and mental health of herself and the baby. This might mean eliminating favorite foods, and restriction of physical activities in accordance with the doctor's advice. The husband also shows his love for his wife and child in many different ways. He is quick to remind the wife of the doctor's orders, to help her with the chores. As an understanding husband he is able to sympathize with and understand the moods and feelings of the expectant mother, even to the point of rushing around to buy pickles when she unaccountably craves them.

Divine Love

"A baby is born of divine love." God takes a very active part in the conception of a baby. A baby is really the work of three lovers: God, the father, and the mother. Human love prepares the human body, but it is only divine creative love that unites the human soul to the human body to form this individual person. The soul of the baby is created at the moment when the human love of the father and mother have prepared the body.

God's love is also active during the months when the mother's body serves as the tabernacle for the baby. Only divine power could place in the single cell the amazing ability to develop into such a highly complicated and organized being as a human body. A book, recommended by your doctor, will help you to understand the gradual development of the bone structure, the heart, the muscular and nervous systems, and the external organs. The mother of the Maccabees expresses what all mothers feel: "I know not how you were formed in my womb; for I neither gave you breath, nor soul nor life, neither did I frame the limbs of every one of you . . . it is the Creator of the world who shapes each man's beginning . . ." (2 Mc 7:22-23).

God's Masterpiece

"A baby receives many great gifts from God." He unites in himself all the perfections of the nonliving and living world beneath him. The human person is midway between the animal kingdom and the angelic realm. He is made of a soul and body into the uniqueness of this human person. Each baby reflects back in his own personal way some of the unlimited perfections of almighty God, his Creator. He has a distinct love and worship to give to God which he alone can give.

The soul is completely indestructible and eternal. Once it has come forth from the creative hand of God it will never die. No hydrogen bomb will ever obliterate it; no germ will ever penetrate and destroy it. The baby will never die even though his body will die. The soul will live and the body will be reunited with the soul to form the complete person at the end of time. The human person has a mind to know truth and a will to love. He has the ability to choose and to choose freely to love or not to love. God also raises the child to be not merely his creature but his son or daughter. Through sanctifying grace the person is united to Christ and in Christ becomes a child of God. He is filled with the life and the love of God.

Destined for Heaven

"A baby is destined for heaven." God loves every human person that he created and died to save, and he wants him to be with him in heaven. Man is made to know and possess perfect truth and to love perfect good. God is perfect truth and goodness, and heaven is union with God. In heaven there is no pain, no sorrow, no parting but only everlasting joy and happiness. This joy is meant to be a family affair shared with father, mother, brothers, and sisters.

Child Discipline

There is so much that could be written about the care and training of your child. Here are some thoughts on the basis of training, which is discipline. "Discipline is the teaching and training of a child so that he will gradually assume his responsibilities to God, self, and his fellow-men."

Teaching

This is the first and most important point in the definition. Discipline means learning, and learning implies a teacher who imparts knowledge. A baby is not born with a storehouse of knowledge but with the ability to learn. The first ideas that the baby receives will come from you, the parents. A child's attitudes, standards, and values will be formed by what he learns from you. Parents do this by anticipating the needs of the child, by answering questions, and above all by example. A child responds more to what parents do than what they say.

Training

It is training that makes teaching a practical part of a baby's life. Teaching may remain sterile without any real influence but training helps a child live according to what he has been taught. This means that the child must be helped to acquire good habits of thinking and acting. Good habits are not acquired by one action but by repeated actions. Skill does not come with the first try, but with many attempts that gradually become easier and more perfect. Habits become second nature so that, as it were, a groove is worn into the personality which enables him to perform certain tasks with ease and smoothness.

To Assume Responsibilities

This is the goal of all discipline, to help a child become a self-responsible adult. True discipline eventually makes the parents unnecessary. If you do your job well, you work yourself out of a job because the child has become an adult who depends on himself. A child must be helped to grow to adulthood not only physically but also mentally and emotionally. Parents who make a child depend completely on them are failing in their task. This assumption of responsibilities must be gradual so that he depends less and less upon his parents. A mature individual is one who has developed a sense of responsibility. There is danger in trying to keep him a baby too long, or to make him an adult too soon. The training must be gradual and adapted to the individual's age and capabilities.

To God

Discipline is a means to an end and derives all its meaning from the goal for which the child is prepared. If the objective of discipline is not clear, then discipline itself will be confused and floundering. If parents do not know the end of the journey, they cannot prepare the child to take the steps on the road to the end. The child must learn in many different ways that the goal of all individual and group life is God the first Creator and the last End.

Responsibility to Self

A child must assume responsibilities not only to God but also to self. He has capabilities of thinking, willing, and doing and must be trained. There must be control established so that he does not give in to every whim or impulse that comes to mind. He must learn to think before he acts or talks, but control does not mean suppression. Part of discipline is to recognize that emotions and feelings have a very definite part to play in an integrated personality. The one who gives in completely to them or the one who suppresses them is not a full, mature person. The child must learn to like himself and forgive himself. If he does not like himself he cannot like others. Self-love is tremendously important, and responsibility means to accept oneself as one really is. This realism does not allow one to deceive himself by thinking he is different than he really is; nor does it make him dependent on the opinions of others to find out his true value.

Responsibility to Fellow-men

A child is not a hermit but a social being who is meant to live in the company of others. He has certain needs and capabilities that require other persons for their fulfillment. Lacking this he will become a selfish person who never has room in himself for anyone else. All of his thoughts will be about himself and he will regard other people not as persons but as things to be used or enjoyed — using them in a way that leaves no respect for them as individuals. Incidentally, an unhappy person — no matter what vocation he follows — is always the selfish person who thinks only of himself, his joys and sorrows; he cannot bridge the chasm between himself and others. He thinks of himself and finds himself and discovers that he is a very miserable and narrow person.

Methods of Discipline

There are two opposite ways of training and disciplining a child: the authoritarian way, with its emphasis on strictness and obedience; and the democratic or permissive way, with its stress on self-determination. In between are many combinations of these two methods.

Too Strict

Those who advocate the firm hand contend that the child needs to learn obedience and control by a method of close supervision and direction. This does produce in general a more orderly home, but there are great dangers involved in too great strictness.

The child can react to great strictness in several different ways. He might go along completely with the firmness and the parent determination theory and thus become a very passive, shy, and dependent child without self-confidence or the ability to make decisions for himself. Such a child would never mature as an adult and would look for a husband or wife who would take the place of the strict parent.

Or a child may openly rebel in word and deed against such strictness on the part of his parents. As a rebel he will refuse to obey even in the smallest matters and will deliberately do just the opposite of what he is told to do. Even things that he would do ordinarily would not be done because they were commanded. Or the rebellion may be inward — outward conformity but inward rebellion. This leads to terrible frustration in the child, great dislike of order and a deep hatred of the parents. This spirit of rebellion can be turned against all authority throughout life.

Too Lenient

Nor on the other hand is too great leniency the proper way to discipline a child. This method insists that a child be allowed a very loose rein so that he can learn things for himself. The emphasis is that he will become a mature individual by learning and making decisions by and for himself. But the precise point of being a child is that the child is not ready for self-control. The child needs principles and rules for guidance and really wants to know what is expected of him. The child is aware, even at times when he doesn't seem to be, of his own inexperience and insufficiency. He will look to the parents for guidance and if you do not offer guidance he will be bewildered and confused. The child wants the security that comes from rules, from knowing what is expected. School children will admit that if they had to make a choice between a completely permissive teacher and one who gave them definite rules for them to follow, they would prefer the latter. Children want to know where they stand and what is expected of them so that they can act accordingly.

Selfishness is another product of too much leniency. An early lack of control allows the child to do only what he wants to do without any concern for others. The child who thinks only of himself from infancy on will never be able to have a meaningful relationship with others. Maturity will not be there. Such a child would be a very poor risk in any of the three vocations of life. Confusion and selfishness are the normal results of too little control!

Best Way

The best method is a combination of the authoritative and the permissive. It is a child-centered discipline in which the needs of the child are the gauge of the discipline. An eminent authority in the field of child psychology, Doctor Arnold Gesell, uses the phrase "developmental discipline" to describe this method. This means that the parent teaches and trains the child according to the stage of his development. Thus the needs of the child, not the needs of the parents, are the prime considerations. The parent demands of the child just as much as he is capable of doing, not too much nor too little, not too soon nor too late.

A word of caution is in line here. Child-centered discipline does not mean that you merely allow the child to go through certain stages without any help from you. It is not good training to say: "Oh, he is just passing through a stage and will outgrow it." No, the function of the parent is to help the child outgrow certain habits and to pass normally and safely through certain stages. Hence you can expect certain stages as the child develops, but you are an important part in each of these stages to help the child pass on to the next stage. There are no bad effects if the parents realize their role as helpers in each stage of child development. The child will outgrow these stages but not without your help.

What About Punishment?

Punishment only enters the picture when the child has done something morally wrong. Then and only then is punishment of some sort in order. But it must be a punishment to fit the crime as well as the personality of the child and the parent. A mere glance or a word may at times be all that a child needs. The child knows that he has done wrong and the mere fact that you know that he has done wrong is enough to bring about a change in conduct.

At other times words or looks are not enough and some sort of action is demanded. It may be that a withdrawal of privileges is a proper answer to the situation. This method has special value when the withdrawal of a privilege is a normal result of the wrong action. Thus a child who violates TV regulations should be denied a favorite program, or a child who is late for meals or who dawdles at the table may find that there is no dessert at the end of the meal.

All thought of punishment raises the matter of corporal punishment on which there is a wide variety of opinions and feelings. Some hold that the rod is still the best method of training; others say that under no condition should a child be spanked; many maintain that spanking can be done under certain circumstances. This could be debated at length but perhaps there is still room at times for some corporal punishment for the young. Sometimes a slap or a spanking at the moment, not afterward, is the only language that a child will understand. But a delayed spanking is not of much value and can even be harmful. In the proper place and proportion physical punishment can do much to help train a child to self-responsibility. If spanking is too frequent, too severe, and the principal method of disciplining, then it is definitely harmful and the offending parent should make a good examination of conscience and resolve to change his thinking and acting.

If the child understands the reason for the punishment, he will accept it. But if he feels that he did not do anything to deserve punishment or that the punishment is out of all proportion to the deed, then punishment will do harm. Above all if the child realizes that punishment comes out of love and concern for him and not out of personal anger, the child will understand and profit. Perhaps not at the moment but later.

There are many joys and sorrows and anxious moments in the raising and education of children. But certainly the joy of family life and the knowledge that a parent is preparing the child for his place in this world and the next one will make the task very worthwhile.

The basic principle is always love and more love for your child.

Kinds of Discipline

There are different kinds of discipline. First there is directive discipline by which the child is guided toward his goal of self-responsibility. The goal of responsibility must be held out and the various means to attain this goal must be given to the child. You must point the way and help the child know where he is going and how to get there.

In relation to others the parent must point out the practice of the two fundamental virtues of charity and justice that regulate all human conduct toward others. Charity enables the child to love others as children of God and to value them as individual persons; justice makes the child respect the rights and property of others. The use of toys can serve as a means of training in both these virtues. In justice the toys belong to the child and the other children's toys belong to them; but in charity the toys should be shared. The child, being inexperienced, is going to continually come to the parents seeking directions for guidance. This can be given in a clear and nondictatorial manner. Suggestion has great value because it helps to make the decisions personal to the child.

There is also corrective discipline when a mistake has been made. Not all mistakes are morally wrong and the child should not be punished unless there has been a mistake made for which he is responsible. In such a case, merely point out the mistake and show how to correct it. Children as well as adults learn from their mistakes. Being young, they will need to be told many, many times. Children often make mistakes because they forget, as their span of retention is very short.

Complaints About Parents

To conclude this chapter, perhaps a little examination of complaints about parents would be in order. Read them with the thought in mind that hopefully they will never be made about you. They are actual complaints made by older people as they looked back over their frustrated childhood.

They did not teach me the principles of religion.

They were too selfish and wanted too much for themselves.

I was blamed for the lack of luxuries in our lives because of the expenditures I caused.

They were too rough and quick with punishments.

They hollered too loudly and cursed and swore.

I was often called dumb and stupid when tasks were not performed to their specifications.

Punishments were out of proportion to the offenses.

They punished me when I told the truth, so I learned to tell lies.

Teaching was always by fear — ''If you don't do this, that will happen!''

They made fun of my attempts to achieve some experience.

My ambitions, my report cards, my choice of work and friends were belittled.

They never let me express my opinions or ideas.

I was overloaded with work and given too much responsibility too early.

There was too much arguing, fighting, brawls, and drunkenness.

They were careless in their intimacies.

No understanding or consideration was given.

Punishment was given for the same things they did themselves, such as swearing, drinking, shirking chores, complaining, poor manners, gossiping, wasting money, and so forth.

They pushed me out of my room in favor of a relative or friend for a long period of time.

I was never given any privacy in my room, bath, or toilet, even in my teens.

Dad was too uncouth in language and manners.

They made many broken promises and too many threats.

They were poor sports, had no sense of humor.

They had no patience in teaching anything and no confidence in me to carry out new ventures.

Mother was a poor housekeeper.

Parents were too crabby, grouchy, irritable, unreachable, aloof, and terribly bad tempered.

chapter 14

money

Money is one of the most serious problems that you must face in your marriage. How much is needed, how is it to be attained, and how is it to be used? Studies reveal that many problems arise in marriages because of money. It puts stress and strain on the personal relationship and makes it difficult for a marriage to survive. Money can be a problem in many different ways: the lack of enough income to cover expenses, the failure to manage and spend wisely, a lack of knowledge about income and expenses, foolish installment buying, a lack of a "we" attitude. Many young couples say that they are never quite out of debt. And payment of bills is always a struggle.

Money is a means to an end, not an end in itself. It should be your slave and not your master. The purpose of money is to provide a family with the necessary and useful things for a decent family life.

Before Marriage

Some clear ideas about the use of money are very important at the beginning of marriage. Many people come to marriage without ever having the experience of fully supporting themselves. During school years parents take care of most if not all of the expenses. If a part-time job was held, the income could not take care of the total cost of education plus the necessities of living. If you worked full-time before marriage and lived at home, the board and room money given to your parents very likely did not cover the full amount. Even if you had an apartment, probably the expenses were shared with others. Of course, if you lived alone, you do have an idea of this difficulty of stretching a pay check to cover rent, clothes, food, utilities, a car, and recreation. It is difficult to earn money and still more difficult to manage it.

Enough to Marry

You must sit down and very honestly figure out if you have enough money to marry. This means not merely enough money to pay for the marriage preparation, but enough money to get a decent start in your life together. First of all it is not wise to bring large personal debts to your marriage so that you have "his," "her," and "our" debts to pay. These debts should be paid off before marriage or at least figured out so that they can be quickly paid after marriage.

You should have a realistic understanding of what it would cost for the basic necessities of rent, food, clothing. Economists say that about a fourth of the income can be spent on housing. A budget or allocation of money should always include something for the many unexpected costs that arise such as repairs to car, sickness, etc. There will be many more unexpected demands on your money than you can foresee.

Standard of Living

In your premarriage talks you should decide upon the standard of living you would like to reach. This must be a realistic goal, one that can be attained by you. Pure dreams without any possibility of fulfillment do more harm than good. Ideals, yes; dreams, no. In setting these goals you must consider the talents and capabilities of the husband as the principal breadwinner and how much you want the wife to contribute to the family income. You realize, of course, that this standard of living is a goal to be worked for, not something to start the marriage with. A man has to be able to know that he can grow and provide a better home for his wife and his family. A wife, too, must feel that better days are ahead. But all in due time.

You realize that you cannot start with the standard of living reached by your parents after many years of marriage. Most couples have to begin marriage at a much lower level than they enjoyed in their parents' home. Usually they have to step down a bit, but they can climb to reach and even surpass the standard of their parents. In this regard, an old but true admonition has great value: "Don't try to keep up with the neighbors." This gets to be a rat race that brings peace neither to the family nor the neighborhood.

The We Attitude

The money you earn is only the first step; the use to which it is put is the all-important second step. Neither husband nor wife should talk about money earned as "mine." It is "ours," to be managed by both of us to cover the cost of living. The husband should tell his wife how much he earns. In our counseling work it surprises us to learn how many wives do not know how much money the husband earns. Communication is surely necessary in this field. To run the home the husband and the wife must know the amount of income, the bills, and the expenses. The income must be stretched to cover the bills and enough set aside to take care of the projected costs of family living. Some sort of budget, or deliberate planning, is necessary in a well-run home. It doesn't really matter whether the husband or the wife writes the checks and pays the bills. This will depend on capability and interest. But the important matter is that both know what is going on and work together. It is good if the wife has a certain amount each week to run the house. Both husband and wife should have money for their own use. Neither should make big expenses without consulting the other. A case in point: One husband bought a house his wife had never seen. (Needless to say this information came to us in our role as marriage counselors!)

Check Your Impulses

Salesmen make a great deal of money by appealing to the impulses of buyers. Items are arranged in an attractive way at a strategic point in a store so that people pick them up even though they really do not need them. Much selling is geared to make people feel they need something that they really don't. The impulse to buy must be controlled by your need of the item and your ability to pay. Money must be used first of all to buy the basic necessities of life — food, clothing, and shelter. Learn how to buy wisely — by price and quality. Recognize true sales by comparative shopping. Perhaps your mothers or friends will have some tips to save you from mistakes they made.

Learn not to give in to the foolish impulses of your partner. Help him realize that you really do not need nor can you afford what he wants. Sometimes young couples bribe each other: "You can have a new hat if I can take guitar lessons." This is only getting your own whim satisfied by gratifying the whim of the other. This road leads only to useless expenses which prevent you from reaching the standard of living you set out for yourselves.

The Husband's Work

The choice of the nature and place of the husband's work can be a very delicate matter. The needs of both the husband and wife must be consulted, but basically the decision belongs to the husband. He must be satisfied with his work if he is to be satisfied with himself. A man is really a bigamist at heart; he has two loves, his family and his work. He works not only to support his family but also to fulfill himself as a man.

It is a wise wife who realizes that she must be satisfied with the job that satisfies her husband. She can help build his confidence so that he might continue to better himself, but she must resist the temptation to nag (constantly insist) that he do so. A man who is not happy with his work is not happy with himself, his wife, or his family. It is an almost impossible burden to live with an unhappy husband, as his unhappiness must hurt those closest to him — his wife and children. If a husband feels that he must make his living in his own business or by selling on a commission basis, the wife must be determined to accept the time spent away from the family and the uncertainties of the family income. Of course, if his own business or his selling does not support the family, the husband must find different work no matter what his feelings are.

Installment Buying

Some young couples become hopelessly caught in installment buying. They have no knowledge of the real rate of interest, nor do they seem to realize that many small weekly or monthly payments blend into a sum that they cannot pay. Installment buying is a part of our American way of life and often is the only way a young couple can buy things they really need. But care and prudence must be used so that only needed items and those that can be paid for are bought. Also you should be careful in making small loans which are so easy to sign and so hard to pay.

Insurance

The proper kind of insurance should give protection for the future. By paying small premiums you can provide for possible emergencies to any member of the family. Some provision should be made for the wife and children in case of the death or disability of the husband. Health insurance is needed because a serious illness can be so expensive that a family can be placed hopelessly in debt. A trusted insurance salesman will present a plan suited to your needs and budget. He will not try to oversell. Also, if possible, there should be some savings, even if it amounts to only a dollar or two put aside each payday to take care of emergencies.

Money and Relatives

Often the question arises as to how much financial assistance the young couple should accept from their parents. This is a very sensitive area particularly when the husband's or wife's family has some money that they wish to give to them. It is a very delicate matter in which the young couple should learn to stand on their own two feet and yet allow the parents to show their love and concern for them. If the gifts are given without any strings, the couple could accept those that they need. But they cannot become too dependent on their parents. A husband's pride is easily hurt if his wife quickly runs to parents for money or gifts or if she constantly reminds him of the source of gifts received.

A young couple can feel too great a responsibility toward their parents, brothers, and sisters. As a result,

they loan or give them money which they cannot afford to do. In real emergencies, of course, help must be given to those in need. But one's first responsibility is always to one's own family and not to the parents. When there is a true need it calls for delicate consideration and agreement of both the husband and wife as to what is to be done.

Money for Recreation

Some money should be set aside for recreation. The husband and wife alone and together need some break in their routine. No person can follow the same course of action day after day without some change. Recreation really re-creates a person anew so that with a fresh outlook and a lighter spirit he returns to his ordinary form of life. The husband and wife should both be able to have a little money that they can spend on recreation for themselves.

Something should be set aside for an occasional evening out for the husband and wife together. Recreation, in general, in marriage should be together so that a husband and wife can relax and enjoy each other's company. Otherwise they can grow apart from each other and become so bored that they do not have anything to say to each other. It is easy to learn how to talk away from the family in a leisurely atmosphere. Wives, especially, like a meal they don't have to prepare. Other forms of recreation can be chosen according to individual preferences.

Church Money

One of the responsibilities of marriage is to help support the Church, your spiritual home. This, too, should fit somewhere into the budget so that provision is made according to the needs of the parish and your ability to give. Contributions should be made on a regular basis so that you do not neglect this responsibility, and the pastor may budget his income to take care of the expenses of the church and school.

Nothing should be taken for granted in marriage and

this applies to money, its acquisition, and its use. When there is love and knowledge you can squeeze through some very lean times without too much strain on your marriage. Use money intelligently and try to have a budget or a planned program for the proper expenditure of money. According to individual differences, families can work from a detailed or general program.

Money will be used properly if used together; money problems will be solved if met together, as is evident when both partners continue to work after marriage.

chapter 15
the working couple

It is to be expected that, at least in early marriage, every couple will go through a time when both partners are employed, perhaps even equally employed. With today's critical economic situation and with the increased public awareness toward a woman's contribution to society and the family, this should no longer be looked upon as an unnatural situation. It would be the better part of wisdom that young girls looking toward marriage not neglect their own self-development. A woman should rightly enter her marriage prepared culturally and educationally for a future that will include not only the raising of children but competence in a line which is in keeping with her own unique talents and abilities — whether this be in a professional or secretarial position does not matter.

The important thing is that she should be prepared to "pick up the ball and run with it" any time the home situation calls for it. Her ability as a mother — given the proper preparation — will be instinctive, inherent, and in love she will be able to fulfill her parental responsibilities well. But her ability in the job market will take some self-knowledge and more intensive preparation. Education or training should be undertaken as a serious step in her preparation for marriage as well as for life. Her employment before marriage and in early marriage should not be looked upon as "just any old job" to pass the time until she settles down to her husband and children. It should be a realization of her potential as a woman.

Advantages of a Working Couple

In spite of all the former objections to a wife's working, there are many advantages which working couples have over those who begin marriage in the traditional roles — the wife remaining at home while the husband works to support her. Of course, the financial advantages at a time when extra expenses are necessary and when a young man is just getting started on his career would be the first and most obvious thing we might mention. But financial security can come in many ways, and not every couple starts out marriage in need of two pay checks.

If there is no economic need, should the wife still consider working? Many say that she should, for there are many intangible yet enduring effects which will come of these years of working together which can only be found in the true partnership conditions which exist for the working couple. When both members of a marriage are engaged in working positions, the traditional roles are temporarily set aside and an equality of persons exists. Given this condition, couples discover the personhood of one another. This is a woman with a talent of her own and this is a man with a career in the making. Each complements the other. They look upon themselves, not just as "he/provider, she/housewife," but as individuals joined in reaching a shared goal — that of establishing a secure future for themselves and their children. They will be sharing more fully in this future and in the plans, decisions, and economy necessary in providing for it.

Sharing Home Responsibilities

The couple will also share in the responsibilities of the home. The wife who works in early marriage and is still expected to do everything necessary to keep the home in order, prepare the meals, and do the laundry, will soon tire of her double role; and the partnership, which was never a true partnership to begin with, is likely to end in resentment. But it is not only for her sake that the household duties should be shared. The husband has much to gain if he becomes familiar with the duties which may, in time, be more totally relegated to his wife. There are bound to be times in their lives when he, also, will have to "pick up the ball" as far as these home chores are concerned. His early experiences will serve him in good stead when these emergencies arise at a later time. But even if it never becomes necessary for him to "fill in" for his wife, the understanding and insight he will gain will have a strengthening effect on their relationship.

There Will Be Problems

It would not be fair to mention the advantages of a working couple without also covering the disadvantages — and there will be many. For one thing, although our society has come a long way in its acceptance of this situation, most young men have been raised in homes where their mothers never worked outside of the home, and where the traditional roles were strictly played out. It will be difficult for young men of this background to accept the sharing of roles necessary for a working arrangement. Although she will, justifiably, expect that he will share in the household chores on an equal basis, chances are that she will be lucky for any little help he may give. Perhaps, on her part, she will do well to settle for this. Otherwise the home could become a battleground over something as petty as housework.

Compromise, however, will go two ways. He will have to learn that the cleanliness of a house is less important than, perhaps, his mother trained him to think. Both of them will also have to relinquish meals that would take all day to prepare in favor of packaged or convenient foods. This can be less of a problem if one really special menu is planned each weekend. And for a greater sharing experience, husband and wife might try alternating the cooking schedule of these weekends. Who knows, he may become a real gourmet cook.

It costs money for a wife to work. A couple's budget must take this into consideration. A woman needs more clothes, necessary convenience foods are more expensive, each must bring or buy a lunch, transportation is a major expense, etc. These problems should be resolved before the marriage or before the wife goes out to work. The working capital which the couple will have to deal with will not be her pay plus his, but her pay plus his — *minus* the added expense of her employment. If the budget is going to be badly strained by these expenses, and if her employment will not add enough to cover them, it might be well to reconsider the wisdom of her working. But before deciding it will not be worth it, some consideration of the future should be allowed.

Emergencies Do Happen

We cannot say to any couple that there will always be a clear path to follow in which each will fulfill his/her traditional role and that the days of their lives will be played out in these roles. Emergencies do happen and the couple who are prepared for them educationally and emotionally will be far better equipped to weather them. The woman who has never worked in her life, who has never prepared herself for any career, will be at the mercy of fate. She will be forced to accept any available position should anything happen to her husband or his working abilities, and she will find herself working for something less than half of what is needed to keep the family going until the emergency has passed. The husband, on the other hand, who has never done the laundry, made a meal, or vacuumed a rug will find himself in a pretty sticky situation should his wife become hospitalized for a time.

When the Husband Is Unemployed

There is also a special kind of emergency unique to our times. It has become more and more a reality in these days of high unemployment. Even well-educated young men are finding it difficult to obtain work. When a wife must work because her husband is unemployed she faces a double challenge — that of keeping the finances in control until he finds work, plus that of helping him to maintain his balance and confidence. If this couple have already had the experience of role-reversal or role-sharing in their early marriage, they will be less apt to fall into the ego-destruction which so often happens during this situation. If a husband knows that his wife can handle her position without great difficulty and if a wife has confidence in his management of the home, the greatest obstacle has been removed — that of self-recrimination on his part, resentment on hers. The husband will be more at ease with this situation which was not of his own making. He will be less apt to feel guilty and more comfortable in that dreadful search-and-wait period which accompanies unemployment. She has worked before, she is good at her job, and there is no element of shame in what she is doing. She, at the same time, must maintain this image, encourage his search, and re-create the partnership of love which they experienced in their earlier days.

The Widowed Mother

God moves in ways unfathomable to man and often we see young women widowed while their children are still small. Working at this time becomes a necessity and a woman's preparation to fill a responsible position will enable her to see her children through school and sometimes through college. Take a look at the young people whose mothers have been left with the burden of raising a growing family. So often these sons become finer men and husbands and these daughters more productive women and wives. In the example the mother has set, they have grown stronger, recognized the need to be prepared for future tragedy, and matured into a sensitivity which comes from experience — in spite of the handicap of having a mother who had to work to support them. Sad as this possible eventuality may be, the wife whose marriage began with a working relationship between her husband and her career will be better equipped to see it through.

While the Children Are Growing

During the years that her children are very young and their needs are great, a woman becomes perhaps a little more mother than wife. The needs of the little ones are demanding and the rewards of watching them grow are fulfilling. She needs little more than this fulfillment and the loving understanding of her husband to complete her world. Very few mothers of small children would exchange roles with anyone. This is what she is created for and the happiness of those years is beyond measure. But this, too, will be a temporary situation. Self-actualization and self-fulfillment are important concepts in the development of a healthy personality, and during the years when her prime consideration is her family's needs, these things are temporarily shelved or experienced from a different angle. It would be a good plan for young mothers to keep in the back of their minds that, somehow, the practice of talents should be continued even throughout these hectic, child-raising years. Reading, studying, keeping one's knowledge up-to-date, and, if the woman has had professional skills, regular contact and practice in these skills should be planned into that busy schedule. For future happiness, the abilities she possesses should not be allowed to stagnate.

And in the Later Years

It happens to every woman, yet it comes always as a new experience. One day she wakes up to discover that the children are growing up and they no longer need her in the same way as they once did. Suddenly she sees the days stretching out before her and the hours of those days threaten her with loneliness and depression. Once again, her early training will aid her in responding to these needs. Once again, in these later years of marriage, husband and wife can become all-in-all to one another. All marriages will not necessarily require that a woman work in her later years, but all marriages should return to this original alliance of joint interest and participation. Marriage should not be a stifling experience but, rather, an experience of growth and mature unity. The woman who has not been socialized to plan for a long life beyond the role of mother to young children faces the danger of becoming the mother who continues to interfere in her children's lives long after their need for her has passed. Even the nonworking woman should create independent activities for herself in her Church or community in order to avoid this common danger. But the confidence and pride which the mature working woman gets from the redevelopment of her personal and unique talents and abilities are pretty hard to match. And it all begins in early marriage when she and her husband worked together for this future end.

chapter 16
relatives and friends

Unless you are an only child and an orphan you will marry into each other's family. Each family has had a great influence in the formation of the individual and still will have some influence, great or small, depending on circumstances. Thus you should have healthy attitudes toward your own family and your partner's.

Giving Away

In the marriage ceremony the father of the bride leads her down the aisle and gives her away to the husband-to-be. This is a very symbolic and meaningful ceremony which stresses the fact that the girl is leaving her parents' home to begin a home of her own with her husband and children. The father, as head of the family, gives the daughter to her husband-to-be in the name of the whole family. Thus the father and the mother, the brothers and the sisters realize that in the true sense of the word they are to take second place in the life of the young bride. The husband-to-be in accepting the arm of the bride signifies that he is assuming his new responsibilities.

Your first love and basic loyalty is to each other and your children. This does not mean that you must stop loving your family. It is not a choice to love either your partner or your family, but to love both your partner and your family. The close love that you have for him helps you to grow in love so that you do have more love to give to your family. It becomes either/or only in a situation where the duties of love are in conflict. With tact and consideration usually the either/or can be changed into and/and. But in case that a definite choice must be made it must be made in favor of the partner. This choice was made on the day of your marriage and should continue during the marriage.

Three Families

In any marriage there are really three families to consider: 1) the family you leave; 2) the family you marry into; 3) the family you begin. Love and consideration can establish the proper relationship between these three families. It is important that proper relationships and practices be developed at the very beginning of the marriage. They should be started during courtship which sets the proper foundations for marriage.

The Basic Problem

Difficulties can arise in marriage when either the older couple interferes or the young couple depends too much on them. It is not easy to bring about a change of attitude in both the parents and the newly married. Old patterns have a tendency to remain and influence the present. It is hard for the parents and the newly married to let go of each other. The marriage ceremony of itself does not do this, but only time and effort effects a proper balance.

A daughter who all her life has turned to her mother must learn to turn to her husband. A son who has always discussed his problems with his father must now discuss them with his wife. A mother who wishes to pass on all her tips on cooking and baby care may find that daughter wishes to run her own home. A mother must be willing to let daughter and especially daughter-in-law learn by their mistakes and offer advice only when it is requested. A father who comes too frequently to repair things at his son's house may find that daughter-in-law does not give him a hearty welcome. Parents must realize that the young son or daughter is now grown-up and married to one who has first claim on his/her love.

If one or the other partner has problems in weaning himself or herself from the family, it is important that the other party understand the problem and be patient and helpful. A storm does not effect a weaning but only intensifies the dependence. Where there is love and consideration these problems need not be major ones. But it is very wise to get off to a good start in your relationship with both your families. Patterns that are once established are difficult to break. It is better not to let them get started than to have to break them later. This only leads to hard feelings on both sides.

Privacy

Privacy (and respect for each other's privacy) is a necessary virtue in marriage. The older couple and the young couple should respect each other's privacy. A phone call to announce a visit is a valued courtesy. Unexpected visits can disrupt plans formed by the other couple. Even the husband and wife need privacy so that they are not always together and always doing the same things together. Each must grow as an individual so that each has more to offer the other. This need for privacy is clearly seen when a husband's work is at home. Usually neither the husband nor the wife likes this because they are too close for too many hours each day.

Some possible problems will be discussed in the rest of this chapter.

Visits

People who love each other want to see each other. Hence visits back and forth are in order. In the beginning of the marriage they will be quite frequent, as both the parents and the newly married adjust to the big change in the way of life. Visits should not be set up on a regular basis so that every Sunday the young couple returns to one or the other home. Once this practice is started it is difficult to break. The newlyweds should be able to do what they want on a Sunday without accounting to their parents. As children come the young couple form their own circle of friends and seek different forms of entertainment. A son or daughter should have the privilege of visiting parents without the company or objection of the partner. Visits back and forth should be frequent and friendly without invading privacy.

Holidays can be a problem with two sets of parents to visit. This again depends on the individuals and the customs of the families. It can be worked out so that the older people see the young couple and their children without it being a great burden to either. Holidays should be joyous and not painful to either family. Love and understanding can make holidays days to remember.

Bringing Problems Home

Advice that is always given but often unheeded is not to bring your marriage problems home to mother or father. Some problems are bound to occur in the period of your adjustment to each other. Settle them before minor problems grow into major ones. But don't try to settle them with your parents. Parents find it too hard to take an objective view. Instinctively, they side either with you or — in an effort not to take your part — with your partner. In neither case can they give an objective and unbiased opinion. Besides, a parent may find it difficult to forget what an in-law has said or done. Future meetings can be strained for both the parent and the in-law. You will more easily forget and forgive your partner than your parent will. With the sting of his words or actions fresh in your mind you may rush to your parent and emotionally say things that are better left unsaid. They represent what you feel in a disturbed mood, not what you ordinarily feel about your partner.

If you need advice or an understanding ear, go to a priest who is trained to listen and help you find the answers. Sometimes a marriage counselor is needed. Usually a priest or doctor can refer you to a qualified counselor if they think you need help. But first of all, try to solve the problem by yourselves, if at all possible. A trusted and prudent friend can be of assistance at times. But be careful in running to the neighbors with your problems. Don't look for one who will always agree with you.

Phone Calls

Alexander Graham Bell has been both praised and cursed because of his great invention of the phone. It is an easy means of communication that spans the country in a matter of seconds. Sometimes it is too easy, and a mother can keep her daughter tied to her apron strings by means of the telephone wire. Daughter is expected to call every day and report, or mother calls every day to learn what is going on. These duty calls become a great problem and are further means of keeping the daughter or the son in subservience. Phone calls should not be too frequent nor too long, so that they are a joy and not a burden.

Baby-sitting

A mother and a mother-in-law suddenly take on new dignity when they become grandmothers. This creates dignity when they become grandmothers. This creates new situations that call for adjustment, especially in the baby-sitting department. This, again, depends on individual situations. You don't want the grandma to baby-sit too much, otherwise she will take over and raise the child. Grandmothers are allowed to spoil children because children need a little spoiling, and it is a grandmother's privilege to do so. Also grandmothers can be imposed upon if asked to baby-sit too often and offended if not asked frequently enough. But there are grandmothers who do not want to take care of the baby because they feel that they have done their work in raising their children. They feel that their children should raise their own. This position is surely understandable and a mutual understanding must be worked out between grandmother and mother. It is good to get things in the open so that each knows where the other stands. It could happen that a mother does not ask grandmother to baby-sit because she does not wish to impose on her good nature, and the grandmother is hurt because she thinks the mother does not trust her with the baby. These and so many other situations can be avoided if there is real communication.

Friends

It is worthwhile to say a few words about friends. Friends played an important part in your life before marriage; their presence at the marriage added to the joy of your wedding day; their friendship can be a great help in marriage. The young couple cannot remain alone and be happy, as every human person needs others in order to develop as a person and a husband or wife. But what friends should be retained and what new friends should be made? Surely some friendships formed before marriage should be kept.

It is not wise to keep only the friends of one of the partners so that, for instance, a husband would not keep any of his friends but adopt the friends of his wife. This is too one-sided and anything one-sided is wrong in marriage.

It is important that both partners be allowed to retain some of their friends that they knew before their marriage. Perhaps they can fit into the framework of their married life and become mutual friends. A wife should be allowed to keep her school and work friendships and have a bridge game or just a talkfest if she wishes. A man should be allowed to have a night out with the boys. But in general most recreation should be taken together. A husband and wife just cannot become a carbon copy of each other. You must retain your own individuality, and this means keeping, in some instances, your friends. By contact with your partner and children — along with mutual friends — you come to full growth as a mature human being. Any growth as a person has to show in your basic relationships with your family.

Your marriage should include a good relationship with others. Your family is only a part of the larger human family of relatives and friends. You need family and friends and they need you.

chapter 17
religion in your home

You will begin your marriage with a religious ceremony in the church not only because it is a beautiful way to begin marriage but because religion has meaning for you. You want God to be present to bless your love as you stand before his altar. Christ will be present in the renewal of his sacrifice of love in the Mass and in the sacrament of Matrimony which you will give to each other. Christ will be as close to you as he was to the young couple at Cana. He comes into your life in the sacrament of Matrimony and wishes to remain there. As you walk down the aisle after your wedding you will just be beginning to live the sacrament of Matrimony.

Thus religion is in every act of your marriage, the big as well as the small signs of love for each other, and the heroic as well as the monotonous duties that lie ahead. And experience teaches that a home in which both the father and the mother believe and practice the same religion is a much happier home than one in which each follows a different religion. This also holds true if one is a practicing member of the Church and the other a nonpracticing member. Once there is a separation from each other in the fundamental views, principles, and moral norms of life it is easy to disagree in other less important areas.

Since religion is so important you must be sure that you and your partner discuss this matter thoroughly before marriage. Attitudes and practices should be understood long before the wedding day. It is too late to discover basic differences only after marriage. This discussion is very necessary if you and your partner are of different religions. Questions about church attendance, education of the children, and freedom to practice one's religion should be examined and an agreement reached. Even if both you and your partner have the same religious faith and regularly attend the same church you should be certain that one is not merely conforming to please the other. This suggestion is in line with the philosophy of never taking anything for granted before marriage.

Call to Holiness

Religion is your relationship with God. The word means the bond that ties you to God and in God to each other. Religion is to "love God with your whole heart, your whole soul, and your whole strength" (See Mk 12:30). It is to become a whole, an integrated person, by becoming holy. Vatican II in its basic document on the Church speaks of "the call of the whole Church to holiness." It emphasizes the fact that not only priests and religious are called to holiness but every Christian who follows Christ. "The Lord Jesus, the divine teacher and model of all perfection, preached holiness of life to each and every one of his disciples, regardless of their situation: 'You therefore are to be perfect, even as your heavenly Father is perfect' '' (Mt 5:48). *(Dogmatic Constitution on the Church,* n. 40).

The Council document applies this universal call to holiness to various groups in the Church. For example: "Married couples and Christian parents should follow their own proper path to holiness by faithful love, sustaining one another in grace throughout the entire length of their lives" (n. 40).

This emphasis on sanctity and perfection is clearly seen in the section on marriage in the *Church in the Modern World.*

"Authentic married love is caught up into divine love and is governed and enriched by Christ's redeeming power and the saving activity of the Church. Thus this love can lead the spouses to God with powerful effect and can aid and strengthen them in the sublime office of being a father or a mother.

"For this reason, Christian spouses have a special sacrament by which they are fortified and receive a kind of consecration in the duties and dignity of their state. By virtue of this sacrament, as spouses fulfill their conjugal and family obligations, they are penetrated with the spirit of Christ. This spirit suffuses their whole lives with faith, hope, and charity. Thus they increasingly advance their own perfection, as well as their mutual sanctification, and hence contribute jointly to the glory of God."

Religion means your bond of union with God and Christ. You are close to God and filled with the spirit of Christ in the sacrament of Matrimony. Perhaps the best way to explain what this implies is to reflect on a sentence which is quoted above.

"The spirit of Christ suffuses their whole lives with faith, hope, and charity."

Faith

With the great gift of faith you will see things not

merely with your human reason but with the wisdom of God. Faith means that you do not see but believe. You take God's word for things precisely because he is God who knows everything and who reveals what is true. Faith, of course, is necessary in all human life, as your human mind is limited and truth is derived from others, for instance the doctor, the lawyer, the merchant, and so forth.

As a Christian, a follower of Christ, you believe that Christ is God. You believe that God sent his only begotten Son into the world to redeem mankind and that Christ is the Sacrament or the Sign of God. A sacrament is something visible, something you see that points to something that you do not see. You are not able to see God, and so God sent his Son to take a human body so that men might see him. When many saw his God-like actions and his God-like conduct and his Resurrection from the dead, they believed that he was what he said he was, the true Son of God.

By your faith you are certain that God sent Christ into the world so that you might become one with him. With Christ you died to sin on the cross and rose to a new life with him on Easter. You now share in the life of the risen and ascended Christ. You are now able not only to have human thoughts but divine thoughts, not only human courage but divine strength, not only human love but divine love. Faith points to heaven or permanent union with Christ as the goal of your life. Your goal must always be above time but must not exclude it because in time you work for eternity. But eternity is your goal and time with its boundaries cannot confine your human spirit. You always want something over and above; you want something permanent and lasting.

The Church

You also believe that the Catholic Church is the sacrament or sign of Christ. You cannot see the risen Christ now, but Christ established the Church to represent himself and make his teaching, his holiness, and his authority present to men and women of all time. Hence the Church points beyond itself to Christ because it is identified with him and brings him to you. Your faith helps you overlook some of the human qualities of the Church and see the divine in the midst of the human. As a follower of Christ you accept the teaching authority of the Church; you frequently come in contact with Christ in the sacraments; you obey the laws made by the Church. The Church leads you to Christ who, in turn, brings you to the Father.

Hope

Trust and confidence are so very important in your married life. There are many difficulties to be met, many problems to be solved in the days ahead. In the midst of these difficulties you must be confident that a real solution can be reached. If you do not trust that a solution can be attained, your hands and feet are tied in hopeless paralysis. The opposite extreme is over-confidence in self so that you think that you can do everything alone without need for other human or divine help.

Hope is a twofold confidence in God and in yourself. You must have trust in the abilities God has given you as a person and the assistance that he has promised you. You have a mind that is made to know truth and to direct you. You have a will that is capable of making the decision to do good and avoid evil. God's loving care and powerful help is evident in the fact that he sent his Son to redeem you, that his providence watches over you, that he made unlimited promises to answer your prayers. "Whatsoever you ask in my name shall be given to you." You have every reason to trust in God, to attain heaven, and to fulfill your duties and carry the crosses of your married life.

St. Ignatius has given you a very wonderful axiom in this regard. "Trust as though everything depended on God; work as though everything depended on yourself."

Charity

The greatest of all virtues in your personal life and in your marriage is charity or love of God and love of neighbor. It is a mutual love between yourself and God. God has loved you so much that he has given you everything, your human life, his Son to redeem you, your life in Christ, the Church, the sacraments, and so forth. Love demands that you give yourself in return. Love, which is the gift of self, always expects the self-gift of the other.

Your response to God is to love him. Your life should not be based upon the fear of God who is seen primarily as a tyrant whose great concern is to punish. The true God is the God of love who desires you to love him and wants you to be united with him in everlasting joy in heaven. It is true that you must fear losing God, but this is rather a fear of losing him whom you love than a negative fear of punishment.

If you love God in this way and show love to your children, they, too, will have a proper love of God. You must realize that your children will form their image of God and of all authority from what they see in you and how you act toward them. Children who are fearful as adults so often come from a home in which love was absent and fear present. If they fear you and if you abuse them, they instinctively feel that this is the way God treats them. They will not be able to reach out to God in love. They will always be more concerned with avoiding sin than with loving and pleasing God. The least imperfection will be magnified into a serious sin.

This love extends to your neighbors. It means that you love God not as an individual but as a member of a community, a group of loving persons, of self-giving persons. Your home, which is your first community, will have an atmosphere of love. Your neighbor is found in all the communities in which you live, your Church, your neighborhood, your city, your state, your world. All of those who share in God's love should receive your love. This means that love cuts through any artificial distinctions of race, color, creed, financial status, and education. Children quickly learn love because it is natural to them. It is only from you and other adults that they will learn prejudice against any group or individual.

If you love you will also keep the commandments. Love is not merely a matter of words but also of actions. If you love you will try to please the loved one. This is true in your relationship with each other and with God. Hence you will keep the commandments, the first three of which direct you vertically to God and the next seven point you horizontally to your neighbor. You will recognize the authority of the Church and obey the laws that she makes to help you along the path to him.

Family Prayer

Family prayer is a wonderful experience which draws members of a family closer to God and to each other. Prayers before and after meals remind the family of the need of gratitude to God, a much forgotten virtue. In a practical sense, it helps promote family unity by allowing the cook to be seated at the beginning of the meal before the others are half finished. Some families pray the rosary or a decade or two at some time in the evening. Other couples say short night prayers together. These and other prayer practices depend so much on individual piety and circumstances, but there should be some common prayer together. You should teach your children some simple prayers and the method of praying informally to God in their own words.

Home Rituals

Religion should be woven into daily living so that it is a normal and natural part of family life. Pictures and statues of Christ, Mary, and patron saints should be found in the home as reminders of Christian truths. These should be not too many so as to cause others to turn away from a too pietistic religion. The art should be good art so that the children learn that good art and good religion can go together. The liturgical season offers many opportunities for home celebrations. The Advent Wreath, the Christmas crib can be made very meaningful to the children.

Education

Your role in the education of your children is well expressed in the documents of Vatican II.

"Since parents have conferred life on their children, they have a most solemn obligation to educate their offspring. Hence, parents must be acknowledged as the first and foremost educators of their children. Their role as educators is so decisive that scarcely anything can compensate for their failure in it. For it devolves on parents to create a family atmosphere so animated with love and reverence for God and men that a well-rounded personal and social development will be fostered among the children. Hence, the family is the first school of those social virtues which every society needs.

"It is particularly in the Christian family, enriched by the grace and the office of the sacrament of Matrimony, that from their earliest years children should be taught, according to the faith received in Baptism, to have a knowledge of God, to worship him, and to love their neighbor. Here, too, they gain their first experience of wholesome human companionship and of the Church. Finally, it is through the family that they are gradually introduced into civic partnership with their fellow-men and into the People of God. Let parents, then, clearly recognize how vital a truly Christian family is for the life and development of God's own people" *(Declaration on Christian Education,* n. 3).

Catholic schools play an important function in the religious formation of children. They assist the home which is the primary school of religion and virtue. "As for Catholic parents, the Council calls to mind their duty to entrust their children to Catholic schools, when and where this is possible, to support such schools to the extent of their ability, and to work along with them for the welfare of their children" (*Declaration on Christian Education*, n. 8).

If attendance at a Catholic school is not possible, you should enroll your children at the parish school of religion and take an active interest in their progress.

If religion is an important element in your home, you will all know better the goal of your personal and family life. You will have the various means to strive for the goal. Hence, if God is love, and religion binds you to God and each other, the real bond of unity is love itself. Where God is, there is love and happiness.

Conclusion

This book has been written to help you "know and love" each other in your marriage. It has tried to present what you should know about marriage, about yourself, and life together in your marriage. It has pointed out that you must love God, yourself, your partner, and your children.

About three to four months before you plan to be married consult the pastor of the bride if both of you are Catholic, or the pastor of the Catholic party if only one is Catholic. Then a date and a time can be set for your marriage. No other definite arrangements should be made until you have seen the priest and set the date. The pastor will tell you what Church documents you need and what the requirements of the civil law are about license and blood test.

The authors' wish and prayer is that you may truly know and love each other. In this way you will give happiness to each other and to your children.

Self-evaluation is always a useful means to encourage better performance. At regular intervals it would be a good idea to read over this check list. Instead of scattering your efforts on many different points, select one or two matters in which you will make determined efforts to improve. From time to time change the points for improvement.

A Check List for Husbands and Wives

To help communication and to better your marriage it might be a good idea to ask your partner to go over the list with you.

I. The Husband

As a Man Do I

Assume my role as breadwinner, protector, teacher?

Follow high moral principles?

Recognize that marriage restricts the freedom I had as a single man?

Treat other women as I expect other men to treat my wife or daughter?

Fulfill the responsibilities of my job and strive to get ahead by study and hard work?

Keep myself neat and well-groomed so that my wife can be proud of me?

Make religion important in my life by learning more about it and practicing it better?

Improve myself intellectually by serious reading?

Better myself socially by becoming a good conversationalist?

Take an active part in community activities?

As a Husband Do I

Show my wife signs of affection and tell her very often that I love her?

Remember wedding anniversaries, birthdays, Mother's Day, Valentine Day and special days of importance in our marriage?

Admire her style in clothes and praise her personal accomplishments?

Consult with her about our financial condition?

See to it that there is always enough money in the house for household and personal expenses?

Try to work out a budget with her?

Put some meaning into my kiss on leaving and returning home?

Make my wife and family happy and not afraid to see me come home?

Make sex an act of love?

Provide for her and the children in case of my death?

Treat her relatives and friends kindly and graciously?

Discuss frustrations and differences in an adult fashion with understanding, calmness, and intelligence?

Consult her and take her into my confidence?

Have enough humility and love to seek professional help if our marriage needs it?

Tell or joke about our personal secrets and intimacies?

Readily forgive her human mistakes?

Make sarcastic remarks or act in a grouchy way?

Help her in household tasks? Feed the baby? Change diapers? Wash dishes?

Thoughtlessly tease too much?

Show leadership in religious practices, family prayers, and devotions?

Act as a good host to her relatives and friends?

Gamble with money needed for the welfare of the family?

Drink excessively and cause unnecessary worry and trouble?

Misinterpret her attention to detail as nagging?

Date my wife by taking her out to dinner, shows, dances, etc.?

Thank her for the many big and little things she does for me?

As a Father Do I

Know and exercise my responsibilities concerning discipline, guidance, affection, companionship?

Help prepare our children for life?

Make myself approachable so that the children come with confidences and problems?

Try to provide a home so that the children will want to bring their friends?

Greet their friends with kindness and respect? Embarrass the children before their friends?

Instill respect for all authority in the Church and in the State?

Promote family recreation such as picnics, outings, tours of historical spots, museums, and so forth?

Take a genuine interest in their schoolwork, games, and other activities?

Praise, compliment, and correct with kindness and understanding?

Tell the children the facts of sex and especially instill the proper attitude toward it? Or leave this duty entirely to my wife?

Support my wife's disciplinary decisions?

II. The Wife

As a Woman Do I

Remember my dignity as a woman and the tremendous power of love that I have to give?

Realize that I am guide, comforter, teacher, nurse, bookkeeper, judge, spiritual director, mother confessor, cook, seamstress, housekeeper, buyer, banker, and entertainer?

Strive to develop my personality and live according to high principles?

Take pride in my work and strive to do it well?

Read good books and magazines, make efforts to improve myself, keep interested in current events?

As a Wife Do I

Recognize that my role is to complete rather than compete?

Give signs of affection and love to my husband and willingly accept his signs of affection?

Show an interest in his work and the people with whom he works?

Make favorable comments on his appearance and try to improve it by proper maintenance of his clothing and gifts of suitable clothing?

Try to save a little toward a nest egg for the future?

Kiss him when he leaves and returns from work?

Do little things for him to keep alive the fires of love?

Search for his virtues rather than his faults?

Belittle or frustrate his ambitions rather than give the necessary encouragement?

Respect his confidences and not reveal the intimacies

of love?

Try to maintain a cheerful atmosphere in the home?

Stoop to using sex as a weapon to be given if he is a good boy and to be denied if he is a bad boy?

Discuss frustrations and differences in an adult fashion?

Treat his relatives and friends courteously and respectfully?

Consult him in matters of importance about personal matters and points which concern the children, and come to a common decision?

Seek professional guidance if needed?

Avoid all types of open and subtle nagging?

Help him in his business or employment if necessary?

Thank him for the many big and little things he does for me?

See the spiritual value of even routine duties in marriage?

Try to economize and manage the household according to income?

Lie to cover up mistakes?

Have a snappy comeback to sting him whenever he says anything displeasing?

Show generosity in making sacrifices for him?

As a Mother Do I

Know and accept my responsibilities as a mother?

Take care of myself during pregnancy according to the advice of the doctor?

Take good care of the feeding, dressing, bathing, night needs of the baby?

Show firmness and consistency in discipline? Use empty threats? Administer discipline at the time of the offense and not leave it to the father who becomes the big bad bear in the eyes of the children?

Give guidance and example in matters of general behavior, manners, clothes, social graces, respect for property rights of others, prayer and worship habits?

Answer the sex questions of the children simply and truthfully and above all give them the proper attitude toward sex?

Give fair and adequate instruction in preparation for a job and marriage?

Graciously let go of a child when marriage, vocation, or college takes him away from home?

By my openness encourage them to come to me and really listen to what they are saying?

Keep a good house so that the children will want to bring their friends home? Act, talk, and dress so that the children can be proud of me?

Uphold the discipline of teachers, priests, employers, so that the children will develop a healthy respect for authority?

Encourage wholesome companions, literature, movies, entertainment? Show respect for their companions by courtesy and kindness? Show the children that I like their choice of friends?

Burden my children with my health, financial, or marital problems?

Praise, compliment, and correct errors with kindness and understanding?

Discipline them in self-denial so that I do not spoil them by giving them too much?

Make it a habit to attend school functions, presentation of awards, athletic contests, graduations, and other events?

Give the girls ample opportunity to learn the role of a woman at home and at work in today's world?

Assign regular chores to the boys so that they may learn the role of a man in a home?

Instill appreciation of the beauty of motherhood and fatherhood?

Blame the children for my hardships and difficulties and play the role of the martyr?

Permit social or community life to interfere with duties of motherhood?

Show shock or surprise at their questions or confidences?

Try to draw out their opinions on life and honestly discuss serious matters with them so that they profit by my experience in arriving at their own decisions?

Shirk my work and yet demand that the children do their work?

Pray for my loved ones?

Expect little heads to have my wisdom?

Criticize or quarrel with my husband before the children?

Leave the children's religious education entirely to the school?